The Personality of Math

The Personality of Math

A Key to Learning and Teaching Math

Paul A. Wagner
Frank Fair

ROWMAN & LITTLEFIELD
Lanham • Boulder • New York • London

Published by Rowman & Littlefield
An imprint of The Rowman & Littlefield Publishing Group, Inc.
4501 Forbes Boulevard, Suite 200, Lanham, Maryland 20706
www.rowman.com
86-90 Paul Street, London EC2A 4NE, United Kingdom

Copyright © 2022 by Paul A. Wagner and Frank Fair

All rights reserved. No part of this book may be reproduced in any form or by any electronic or mechanical means, including information storage and retrieval systems, without written permission from the publisher, except by a reviewer who may quote passages in a review.

British Library Cataloguing in Publication Information Available

Library of Congress Cataloging-in-Publication Data Available

ISBN 978-1-4758-6297-3 (cloth) | ISBN 978-1-4758-6298-0 (pbk.) | ISBN 978-1-4758-6299-7 (ebook)

Contents

Preface	vii
Acknowledgments	ix
Introduction	xiii
Chapter 1: Indoctrination and Genuine Math Education	1
Chapter 2: The Personality of Math	19
Chapter 3: The Human Side of Mathematical Personality	31
Chapter 4: Two Takes on Recent History: Pure vs. Applied Mathematicians and Women in Mathematics	51
Chapter 5: Math Problems and the Personality of Math	65
Chapter 6: Educating for Understanding the Personality of Math	77
Chapter 7: Introducing Students to Mathematics	101
Bibliography	111
Index	125
About the Authors	133

Preface

There is intense interest in making STEM (science, technology, engineering, and mathematics) studies more potent than ever. Developments in curricular content, instructional strategies, and evaluation of success are looked at afresh. Even history and philosophy are recognized as critical to the new STEM awareness, as in the coalition of teacher training programs known as UTeach. By discussing the personality of mathematics, we bring high school teachers and lower division college instructors to an awareness of how they can address these new concerns. We do this by showing them that disciplines have personalities, much as humans and human communities do. This attention to personality is most especially needed in math education.

We accept that math education must contain indoctrinative strategies which instill math facts in students. We also recognize the need for students to have opportunities for hands-on experiences in applying math. But to help students become *very good at math* or even truly just *good at math*, much more is required. Students must learn to pass through thresholds that will bring them into the lively and animated experiences of mathematical reflection and investigation.

Imagine the goal of leading students to becoming very good at math—or better! This becomes the platform supporting all advanced math study, both applied and purely theoretical. This platform sits on three legs, much like the seat of a three-legged stool. One leg of the stool focuses on instilling well-confirmed facts and skills in the minds of students at every level of achievement. A second leg of the stool engages students in hands-on operation of mathematical tools within one of the families of applied mathematical operations. Both legs are essential to students becoming good at math or better. But to truly succeed, for students to become optimally competent, a third leg of the stool must be recognized, shaped, and reinforced.

The third leg of the stool comprises the personality of mathematics, which brings in awareness of the history, philosophy, and psychology of math. This is the leg of the platform that this book addresses. Without a focus on this support of the platform, there is little else that can substantially enliven learner efforts to advance in math understanding. There would be much less zeal for pressing on into the math wildernesses themselves, for exploring and revealing new ideal truths and astute applications, applications that have the power to reveal the hidden geometry of all of reality and much of human experience.

Take the journey seriously and sustain students' courage with this third leg of the platform structure, and then they will succeed in deepening their math understanding and do so with well-earned pride of accomplishment.

Acknowledgments

PAUL WAGNER

First and foremost, I want to acknowledge my co-author. He is so much more than an able philosopher and scholar. He has an uncommon sense of compassion and duty toward all he encounters. Without going into detail, he is the man every spouse and family would cherish as one of its own. In addition, there is a reason why he is a distinguished emeritus from his university. Beyond scholarship, he has won teaching awards that give him an uncommon instinct in what we write about here. His teaching and scholarship have crossed the disciplinary boundaries of four colleges within the university. He has carried disproportionately heavy loads of editing responsibilities for journals. More than a pleasure, it has been an honor to work with him.

Second is the deceased polymath Patrick Suppes of Stanford University. Suppes directed doctoral students in electrical engineering, mathematics, philosophy, psychology, and education. It seemed that within a few minutes Suppes could ask the most penetrating questions and drain my mind of anything I ever learned about a given subject. Known most famously as the Father of Computer-Assisted Instruction, Suppes was a cross-over mathematician from very nearly every angle imaginable. He was a palpable model for nearly every chapter in this book.

Third, Hilary Putnam was a giant in mathematical philosophy. Even as he aged, his eye for even the slightest absence of rigor was impeccable. Math is often said to be a young person's game, but one could see no instance of that in Putnam's ability to see the frayed arguments in any argument about logical truth. As much as anything, I remember Putnam for his gentle reassurances encouraging me that I was on the right track for this or that claim. Putnam's educational experience highlights so much of what this book is about. In Putnam's autobiographical essay included in *The Philosophy of*

Hilary Putnam, the Library of Living Philosophers volume dedicated to him (2015b), Putnam describes how his early ambitions in mathematics were nearly thwarted when he was an undergraduate at University of Pennsylvania considering math as a possible major.

Putnam deferred taking math courses at an undergraduate level because he was "terrified of the idea of solving problems under pressure" (2015b, p. 13). Yet his personality was aligned with the personality of math, just not with the practice of math instruction. Nonetheless, as we suggest in this book, personality alignment between mathematics and its champions trumps simply being "good at math" on standardized tests. Putnam went on to publish over thirty articles in professional mathematics journals, became a co-founder of formal learning theory, and supervised mathematical dissertations in the math departments of both Harvard and MIT.

Both Suppes and Putnam instance what we have been illustrating all along about the alignment of mathematics and the personality of its champions. This alignment is not something that can be reliably captured through standardized testing, and that should be evident to anyone studying math today (Morrison, 2022, pp 102–104).

FRANK FAIR

Let me reciprocate the generous words of my co-author, Paul Wagner, by acknowledging the simple fact that the idea for this book and the great majority of its substance is due to his work. The breadth of his reading and his ability to synthesize a vast amount of diverse information is, frankly, astonishing to me. And his passion for educational reform is deep and genuine. I am glad to be able to render some assistance along the way.

I should also acknowledge those who first introduced me to symbolic logic and, eventually, to set theory and a deeper understanding of calculus than I had when I first took calculus long, long ago as a college freshman. The first person who introduced me to symbolic logic was Edward MacKinnon, and, in a nice connection with this project, the text we used was by Patrick Suppes. The second person is Bowman Clarke, who led me through multiple axiomatic systems, who read Quine's *Set Theory and Its Logic* with me, and who, not least, directed my dissertation on erotetic logic, the logic of questions.

Finally, I should mention a text, *First Order Mathematical Logic,* by Angelo Margaris that was my introduction to the work of Georg Cantor, his diagonal argument in particular. It blew my mind on first encounter, and it was a clear demonstration of creative genius and persistence in asking deeply probing questions and in being able answer those questions by providing genuine proofs of what seem at first glance to be "crazy" ideas.

Introduction

The mathematician Edward Frenkel expresses our concern very eloquently in his *Love and Math: The Heart of Hidden Reality* when he writes the following: "What if at school you had to take an 'art class' in which you were only taught how to paint a fence? What if you were never shown the paintings of Leonardo da Vinci and Picasso. Would that make you appreciate art? . . . [B]ut this is how math is taught, and so in the eyes of most of us it becomes the equivalent of watching paint dry" (Frenkel, 2013, p. 1). As the title of our book indicates, we believe that engaging with the personality of math is an essential key to learning and teaching math.

Remember that, when we look at history, we learn, for example, that Muslim students were taught nearly 1,300 years ago to entertain mathematical puzzles about the movements of the heavens. Jewish children have long been taught to consider puzzles in the Torah, and rabbinical commentary evolved over the centuries to address these puzzles. In Ancient Greece the Pythagoreans were enamored with the idea that numbers were the language of a Creator and the key to understanding the universe. Socrates provoked the citizens of Athens to look past the obvious and question more deeply what might be afoot in any ordinary human judgment, and his student, Plato, celebrated the ability of math to give us truths about ideal objects existing beyond sense perception.

Amartya Sen points out that there were seeds of voting mathematics in early Indian writings of over two millennia ago, and the Chinese from Confucius to Lao Tzu pondered paradoxes of all sorts. In short, from around the world cultures were led to various levels of success because they had within them thinkers who raised questions and developed conceptual tools to probe deeper into matters that most other people never imagined. All these thinkers were engaged in some aspect of reflective deliberation and critico-creative thinking.

Such thinking, particularly when aligned with mathematical reflection, is found among all peoples and people of all ages. We begin in wonder, we advance through analysis, and, if we succeed, we construct plausible new accounts of the world surrounding us. This work of wonder, analysis, and sometime successful production of novel insights, has been embodied across all cultures in what rightly may be called "The Great Conversation of Humankind."

When Harvard psychiatrist Robert Coles travelled throughout Africa, India, China, and the United States, he found children five to nine years old universally inclined to ponder how people should treat one another and ponder as well whether or not there is a hereafter, an initial creator or act of creation, a universal construction of all that exists, and other metaphysical puzzlements (Coles, 1991).

The Director Emeritus of the Max Planck Institute for Human Development, Gerd Gigerenzer, has demonstrated that children as young as five or six are interested in risk analysis and naturally disposed to doing it a bit better with each try (Gigerenzer, 2015). Risk analysis can be thought of as the appropriation of technical tools from philosophy and mathematics to aid persons in figuring their way around the world.

Aristotle thought humans were rational by nature. In contemporary terms we might say similarly that evolution seems to have prepared human beings for deep reflection and analysis, and this is repeatedly demonstrated in our collective participation in the Great Conversation of Humankind. Educators must build on that natural impulse.

Too often, educators worry about how they might motivate students to learn. Our sense is that that is the wrong question. The right question is to ask, "What are we doing to drive the natural instinct to learn away from students?" Evolution crafted humans to engage in ever more reflective and deliberative mental activity.

Pop culture, the media, and many current education practices of inept schooling seem to mitigate against the exercise of deliberative and reflective thinking. Clearly, educators must free students to re-engage wonder. Wonder thrives in social contexts that encourage participants in the earnest search for truth. Analysis, speculation, and hypothesizing each nurture the unmitigated search for greater understanding in the human species' Great Conversation.

Truth is a key concept and an ideal in the Great Conversation. Math is an especially liberating example of success in truth-seeking, and it fosters the indispensable hope for truth securing. The hope for securing mathematical truth prompts the search for knowledge, a search for a set of privileged propositions and inferential regulatory practices that eliminate previous errors and presumably clear the way to approaching further truth.

The tools for restoring students' intellectual freedom are available, but they most especially do not include endless preparation for standardized tests. As Nobel Laureate in physics Richard Feynman famously opined, "The path to the Nobel prize in any science begins with a question relentlessly pursued." Or, as we would like to put it: *Intellectual freedom begins by recognizing it is doubt, not fact recognition, that liberates the mind from intellectual complacency.* In contrast, training for multiple-choice standardized tests induces complacency.

When the student does not understand, schooling (as opposed to genuine education) discredits the adventure of learning by using student time to teach gimmicks for answering multiple-choice items. Single-minded test preparation, in math especially, destroys wonder and any sense of adventure when exploring questions whose answers are often far from obvious.

Shared deliberation and constructive criticism advance the common cause of understanding. Shared deliberation involves knowing how to question. Answers naturally follow skilled questioning practices. Shared deliberation involves knowing when and how to use possible counterexamples to confirm, abort, or at least avoid prematurely discarding novel conclusions.

Schooling may too often be satisfied with adequate test scores and students' ability to deliver teacher-favored platitudes when solicited, but all this must give way to the educational ideal of developing in students the ability to create detailed explanations—if there is to be any real understanding. How many students can guess rightly an answer to a question pertaining to the Pythagorean theorem, but, at the same time, may have no real understanding of the theorem until they began work as a carpet layer, roofer, architect, or engineer?

In the pages that follow there will be no one-size-fits-all solution to test achievement. Rather, the emphasis is on understanding a community of people so engaged in mathematics as to find some personal identity with its natural beauty and allure. The problems of mathematics are illustrated to reveal their charm—as opposed to a demand for the replication of an answer in order to allegedly chart accountability. Accountability in math education is most evident when students want to learn some other plays in the expanding rule book and strategic practices of math play. This book provides abundant illustrations for initiating students into the mathematical aspects of the Great Conversation and the personality of math as revealed through that aspect of the Great Conversation.

The title of chapter 1, "Indoctrination and Genuine Math Education," suggests a role for what can be called "indoctrination" in math education. A student must acquire basic facts ("say this as I say it"; "do this as I do it") along with mechanical skills to begin progress in mathematical operations. For example, a student who does not know how to add and subtract cannot learn calculus.

Admittedly, as previously noted, there is a danger of settling for "successful indoctrination" that is easily and inexpensively measured by performance on standardized tests. Instead, students need to be brought to and through thresholds in math, thresholds that lure them to entertain novel challenges in their approach to the mathematical wilderness. When this happens, they cross the threshold and enter new mathematical terrain. Passage through a threshold, as a criterion of success, is benchmarked by evidence that learners are able and inclined to express *well-grounded doubt* about knowledge claims in various areas of math.

The book continues with chapter 2, "The Personality of Math," which develops the notion of the personality of math. Math, notably, has the ability to organize thought with increasing transparency, and from the Greeks onward its accessibility to proof gives reason to accept its evolving transparencies.

Math is a source of wonderment when people seriously contemplate the notion of infinity and when they are confronted by puzzles such as Hilbert's Hotel and Zeno's paradoxes. Other disciplines also have personalities, but the point is that to genuinely introduce students to math, they need at some point to gain a sense of its distinctive personality.

Chapter 3 addresses "The Human Side of Mathematical Personality" by looking at a number of mathematical heroes from Hypatia in the ancient world to more recent champions of math such as Ramanujan, Claude Shannon, John von Neumann, and Patrick Suppes. One of the main points illustrated in this chapter is that knowing math is not the same as being a mathematical adventurer. The champions of math welcome the adventure that comes with exploring the wilderness of math in order to blaze new trails.

Chapter 4 looks at diversity within the ranks of mathematicians by giving "Two Takes on Recent History: (1) Pure vs. Applied Mathematicians and Women in Mathematics." In the first case, this chapter relates the tension between G. H. Hardy and his student Norbert Wiener, the father of cybernetics, over who could truly count as a mathematician. Hardy was a purist, while Wiener was a math champion who used math to advance our ability to understand and control the natural world.

In the second case, everyone knows of the women's movement for equal rights, but we may be surprised to learn of the civic leadership and fierce sense of public justice exhibited by Hypatia in Alexandria over sixteen hundred years ago or to learn of the efforts of Maria Gaetana Agnesi in the eighteenth century or Sofia Kovalevskaya in the nineteenth century to bring women into respect for their intellectual abilities—all despite male slights and neglect which hindered their progress at every step. The mathematical personality involves courage and persistence.

Chapter 5 is on "Math Problems and the Personality of Math." It describes problems that have played a role in prompting the development of mathematics, problems such as whether Euclid's Fifth Postulate could be proven to be a consequence of the other four, problems involving prime numbers and infinities, and those relating to imaginary numbers.

These challenges reveal mathematics as truly the queen of all searches for reality. Math is a game breeding many smaller games, each and every one of which has the potential to open doors for others to walk through to investigate the unknown (Stewart, 2021, pp. 10–11).

Chapter 6 is "Educating for Understanding and the Personality of Math." This chapter gets to the pedagogical heart of how educators can bring more students on board by developing mathematical resources for investigating and planning in life, in matters both great and impersonal, as well as matters small and personal. It discloses the diversity of mathematicians, including the purists, the champions of applied math, and those who stress the use of math to make our inferences in the other sciences clearer and more secure, the "epistemic champions." A number of examples of each type of math champion are given, both from math's earlier days and from the present.

It shows how math and philosophy must be wed in open discussion to bring students face to face with the possibility that they too might become math lovers or at least more appreciative of aspects of math.

We conclude with chapter 7, "Introducing Students to Mathematics," in which the reader is brought full circle back to the history of mathematics to sum up its personality in order to personalize the encounter students can have with their math education. Courage, a sense of adventure, wonderment, and persistence in the face of impending defeat are all characteristics the math lover needs to surmount challenges, just as athletes on the field need them.

It just may be that teachers, as they learn to be more intimately engaged with the personality of math, can learn how to share more effectively that intimacy with students. Then together all can proceed further in the Great Conversation where mathematics is omnipresent in its ability to turn participants away from the misleading shadows on the cave wall and toward the light of further understanding.

The training required to teach teachers how to use the materials contained herein is not extensive and can easily be included in many teacher-training courses. More importantly, the material in this book will ideally serve every teacher by being kept on the desk in easy reach for that vitally important "teachable moment."

Chapter 1

Indoctrination and Genuine Math Education

[Note that much of the material in this chapter is adapted from Wagner, P. A. (2021), The methods, benefits and limitations of indoctrination in mathematics education. Interchange: A Quarterly Review of Education, 52(1), 41–56.]

MAKING STUDENTS GOOD AT MATH IS NOT THE PROPER AIM OF MATH EDUCATION

This may sound like an odd claim to make, especially in a book that holds math accomplishments and mathematicians in the highest of esteem. The oddness is removed when it becomes evident that the term "good at math" does not represent much of anything very effectual. To begin, the term "good at math" for all intents and purposes represents little more than exceeding one standard deviation above what average students score on an SAT or some other standardized test. This score amounts to little more than some modest skill in calculation, recognition, and maybe some skill at choosing likely answers in response to a multiple-choice item despite knowing perhaps little about the subject. These are hardly traits of mathematical excellence.

In the flurry of interest surrounding deficiencies in STEM subjects, there is a rush to show accountability that students are improving in math and other STEM–related skills. Unfortunately, multiple-choice test measurements will never accomplish the desired goal of showing improvement in mathematical *understanding*. Understanding comes with mastery over some subject. The best that standardized tests in math can measure is ritual adherence to an algorithmic procedure with limited application. In the following chapters, the goal is not to provide yet another set of recommendations for math improvement so more students can boast of being "good at math," but instead the goal is to create space where those with the promise of excellence can find a promising path beyond a mere standardized test score.

In the process there are models, examples, and recommendations that should clear the way for those merely "good at math" to improve their understanding of math, but the primary aim is to open a window so that those with various degrees of mathematical competency can see the incredible vistas that the genuine heroes of math are eager to explore. The talk in much of this book refers to math heroes. These are people in both applied and pure math who see beyond what the solution to a conventional algorithm might lead to in some mechanical sense. Math heroes share personality traits that align with the personality of math itself.

Imagine each traditional academic discipline having something of its own personality. Just as people may be drawn toward particular persons as suitable romantic partners and not toward others for some reasons, so too people seem naturally primed to find welcome in say history, but maybe not math—and vice versa. Each realm of study strongly entrenched in tradition has developed characteristics that may romance new suitors. This is much of the story ahead. In addition, the suitors of a discipline develop personality traits that are analogous to what is naturally aligned with the manifest traits of an academic discipline.

These traits of mathematics and those who are its most successful suitors will be discussed below. To anticipate what lies ahead, consider the following as key traits of both mathematics and those who seek her graces. One is zeal for adventure. Second is a love of creating paths through a previous unknown wilderness. Third is a passionate love for the content of the wilderness ahead. Fourth is the ability to sustain pursuit of what is beloved over an uncommon length of time (here obsession might be a good thing, a virtue). Fifth is an unmitigated esteem for truth and not settling for some mere facsimile. Math demands these traits in her heroes. Her heroes naturally reveal these traits the longer they pursue math excellence.

Math excellence is not what current STEM curriculums, which are subservient to standardized tests, aim for. More often than not they blunt such interests by settling for merely "good at math." Here we open paths into the personality of math for potential heroes to follow. These paths into excellence can also energize those who are merely "good at math" to respect the promise of excellence that heroes are able to share one day.

Being good at math may be an invaluable asset for engineers, but being merely *good at math* will never produce notable pure mathematicians like Leonhard Euler or, in modern times, like Shing-Tung Yau or Grigori Perelman. Nor will being good at math produce notable scientists like Claude Shannon, John von Neumann, John Nash, Amos Tversky, and Stephen J. Gould, nor medical scientists like John Ioannidis or statisticians like Howard

Wainer. So, what does an early path to the edge of mathematical wilderness look like?

COOTIES AND INDOCTRINATION

Some may remember long ago young children did not want to associate with another child or group of children because they had the dreaded "cooties." Now, what were cooties?

Nothing.

Cooties merely designated others that were avoided largely because they were mysterious to the denigrators of cootie possession. Cootie possession ranged from genders, to race, intellectual prowess in school, rich versus poor kids, ethnicity, perhaps religion. Characteristics that the cootie denigrators did not understand, other than knowing they appeared different from one's self and one's friends. Often cootie obsession is something children overcome with age—but not always. The challenges of race, ethnicity, and gender prejudice remain and, in this time of social conscientiousness and justice, are formally addressed by teachers and educational policy.

An age-old solution to the problem of cooties is dressed up in educational jargon, but it remains largely the same strategy that has been used for decades: Get to know those described as having cooties. Why do I have to learn to dance with X, they have cooties? Why do I have to play ball with X, they have cooties? Why do I have to work with those kids, they have cooties?

Each time one of the most effective strategies for addressing fear of cooties was simply to require children to engage one another in prescribed ways until they felt a bit more comfortable with each other. These prescriptions for social engagement were not left up for discussion. They were things that were done to get children beyond their fears and misconceptions about others. These prescriptions were indoctrinative. "Do this in this way!" And then see your world expand and your confidence in dealing with it expand as well.

These strategies work. And they are instances of indoctrination. Too often since the 1940s people are repulsed by the word "indoctrination" before they have given much thought to the strategy or its purpose. This complicates a number of otherwise common-sense strategies for getting things done proficiently. For example, learning to count and to add and subtract are taught in the absence of good reasons addressed to students. Here "do this as I do it" is the alpha and omega of such instruction, much as in the case of English speakers learning the alphabet song.

Indoctrination as historically understood is simply acquiring some habit of belief without being given a simultaneous justification. In the examples above indoctrination makes sense, but when indoctrination becomes excessive it becomes objectionable. Indoctrination is excessive when reasons could accompany an explanation or practice, but they are avoided simply in order to control those indoctrinated. The goal is to produce a mindset to act and believe as instructed and nothing more. In math even the future heroes need, at first, language and practices to extend their number sense toward the frontiers of the math wilderness ahead. In this they are no different from all other children. A bit of indoctrination is unavoidable. And, as for all children, when the threshold of indoctrination is no longer needed, no child should be subjected to it.

MATH EDUCATION FOR ALL UNAVOIDABLY BEGINS WITH A BIT OF INDOCTRINATION

Historically the term "indoctrination" was synonymous with the term "teaching" (Callan & Arena, 2009; Gatchel, 1972; Green, 1972, p. 9). In the Oxford Online Dictionary, for example, the meaning of the noun indoctrination is given as "the process of teaching a person or group to adopt a set of beliefs uncritically" (https://www.lexico.com/en/definition/indoctrination).

Much has changed in the last seventy-five years (Snook, 1972). The public connotation of the word "indoctrination" has deteriorated. There is empirical evidence that teachers have become so fearful of being accused of indoctrination that they single-mindedly focus on the dictates of a standardized rubric which they had no role in developing (Wheeler & Feghali, 1983). Still, simplicity of definition secures clarity (Sober, 2015). Here *indoctrination* is defined *as causing someone to accept a belief or disposition without that person having any current ability—as opposed to a capacity that may be developed later—for justifying that belief.*

This definition does not draw people into convoluted accounts regarding an alleged indoctrinator's state of mind, intentions, truth or falsity of doctrinal utterances, or any other matters except the consequences of identifiable abilities and practices in the person said to be indoctrinated. There is no reason why a *definition* of indoctrination must also entail a criterion for justification. The definition need only identify whether or not indoctrination has taken place (Snook, 1970). Indoctrination can be a useful benchmark term identifying students' responsive mental states (Wagner, 2018, p. 309).

This parsimonious definition of indoctrination allows benchmarking as to whether or not students are developing a feeling for and an understanding of the beliefs and dispositions they are acquiring. This is especially important in mathematics education. Benchmarking indoctrination alerts teachers to when indoctrination occurs. Its benchmarking utility can make educators mindful of when the threshold of indoctrination is breached and thus help educators avoid continuing unnecessary indoctrinating practices.

However, indoctrination is dangerous. It is dangerous not just when it instills unsupportable social, religious, and political beliefs in others, but *it is also and, perhaps especially, dangerous when it suffocates imaginative understanding properly exercised in acquiring new knowledge* (Bailey, 2010; Callan & Arena, 2009; Graham & Kantor, 2009).

When we see the panic of some teachers who are desperate to instill in students facts aligned with standardized, high-stakes tests, it is easy to notice that it is increasingly ubiquitous in much of K–12 education (Landsman & Gorski, 2007; Nichols, Glass, & Berliner, 2012: Ravitch, 2010). Think back to the behavioristic measures students were subjected to in the 1950s and 1960s. Recall subsequent standardizations since the 1990s and the advent of No Child Left Behind (Darling-Hammond, 2007; Koretz, 2008). And, because of continued standardized measurement using test-focused rubrics in math education, sensitivity to the *threshold* of indoctrination's disvalue is increasingly ignored (Chomsky & Robichaud, 2014).

The definition of indoctrination noted above applies arguably to the standardized test-driven shaping of human minds (Callan & Arena, 2009; Bailey, 2010; Siegel, 1989). But, if there are no reliable grounds for knowledge acquisition, then all claims to know are relative to time and place—*even in mathematics* (Zellini, 2020; Butterworth, 1999; Dedekind, 1888)! In short, if all is relative, then there is *no commitment to truth* as an ideal (Harvey, 2004; Putnam, 2015a; Sokal, 2009). Yet the very personality of mathematics embraces truth as an ideal (Spelke, et al., 1992).

ORIGINS OF MATHEMATICAL SCHOOLING

Neuroscientists, along with both evolutionary and developmental psychologists, learned much in the past fifty years about development of the human number sense, developmental patterns, and the effects of dyscalculia (Butterworth & Kovas, 2013; Dehaene, Dehaene-Lambertz, & Cohen,1998; Glimcher, 2004; Devlin, 2000; Gopnik, Meltzoff, & Kuhl, 1999; Kovas et al., 2007). Obviously, humans had to be a certain type of creature with certain cognitive processing abilities to become "number wise" and capable of being trained to understand and advance math thinking forward (Artstein, 2014; DeFilipe, 2011; Gallistell, Gelman, & Cordes, 2006). That being said, the earliest math schooling reveals much about early math learning.

As Ian Hacking explains, "Deep in human thinking is a sense of symmetry . . . intensely investigated by psychologists today. . . . But gradually other inferential mathematical structures proved inviting as well and the nature of math is to follow the possibilities inferential structures alluded to" (Hacking, 2014, p. 171–72).

The very first such schools discovered anywhere in the world are in Mesopotamia and were called "tablet schools." Initially, they taught pictogram symbols for five thousand items. This is not surprising inasmuch as primitive peoples today teach numerical meaning similarly (Tversky, 2019, p. 177). Subsequently, in later generations, students were taught modification and combinatorial strategies and the "alphabet" was reduced finally to two hundred or so symbols with rules for combination (Mlodinow, 2015). There was neither interest in, nor reason for, giving students objectives, creative prompts, or anything of the kind. Initially, it was just a matter of having people know how to record events in ways specified by conventions (Lewis-Williams & Pearce, 2005; Zellini, 2020, pp. 24–26).

The standard story of how and why people learn is usually given in terms of evolutionary need and adaptation (Nirenberg & Nirenberg, 2021; Nieder, 2019; Crow, 1988). But often attributes are developed which subsequently show utility unrelated to previous adaptational needs (Maor, 1991; Nieder, 2020; Tammet, 2012; Tomasello, 2014). This seems to be so with many human cognitive systems.

Brain development outpaced evolutionary pressures at times (Balter, 1998; Curry, 2008; Gallistel, Gelman, & Cordes, 2006). As a consequence, human brains had the opportunity to speculate and wonder as no other animal brains seem to do (Artstein, 2014; Morris & Macedo, 2015). The cost of the rapidly oversizing brain nearly proved lethal for a time; it demanded high energy cost and offered low immediate fitness benefit (Mlodinow, 2015, pp. 12–15).

The human capacity to speculate led to abstraction and imagination. Both would prove useful in generations to come (Alexander, 2014; Poundstone, 1988). Religion is evidence of early imaginative and speculative capacities that are the same capacities required for mathematical thinking (Bradley & Howell, 2011). In short, humans became by nature wondering, speculating, and abstracting animals (Mlodinow, 2015, pp. 20–21). Their emerging academic disciplines began developing personalities of sorts.

Learning to count requires an ability to abstract from what is observed (Butterworth, 1999). Each token number is learned by rote. Initially there could have been no explanations of how tokens are abstract representations. Sharing how to count required indoctrinating efforts imposed on learners by those of greater experience. Indoctrination had to serve as a gateway for learners from instinct to the practice of counting in context (Wiley, 2015, p. 405). But gateways are only an approach and not part of the eventual immersion and then passion for the personality of a discipline.

A brief sketch of mathematical history proves instructive. In the tablet schools of Mesopotamia, pictograms for communicating led to abbreviated forms economizing on symbols. From five thousand symbols originally contrived for numbered observables, a more manageable set of four hundred symbols evolved. These numerical symbols for simple calculation became part of the *context-driven fundamentals* to be learned in this early moment in educational history (Balter, 1998). Context-driven fundamentals are concepts acquired *prior to* an effective focus on an identifiable problem space (Bartha, 2010; Boesch & Tomasello, 1998). One can imagine testing these competencies with the standardized tests of today.

Numerical representation is a context-driven fundamental (Tversky, 2019). But it is dependent on brain mechanisms that must be activated by experience (Dehaene, 2020; Gordon, 2004; Pica et al., 2004). Numerical representation made possible the construction of great cities such as those of the Mayans, Mesopotamia, China, India, and even the pyramids of Egypt (Ifrah, 1985). As long as the goal of mathematical thinking was to construct buildings, enable accounting practices, and improve economic efficiency, abstracting about the abstractions of numbers was not in the cards for centuries to come. The personality of math was still in its infancy.

Since counting and even early operational competencies such as addition and subtraction did not immediately open any doors to mathematical speculation or understanding, early on numerical competency was solely a matter of indoctrination, that is, direct instruction and ritualized signaling (Wiley, 2015). As philosopher Catherine Elgin argues, even today much instruction can be conducted apart from legitimating reasons. Instead, simple sociological practices tell students: "Here, see this. Now, do this as I do this" (Elgin, 2017).

The Pythagoreans of ancient Greece were among the first to speculate about the abstract potency of mathematical thinking. They pushed beyond the pragmatics of "true enough" (Mazur, 2005, pp. 25–27). Pythagoreans sought to weave mathematics into a mystical view of life centering on THE TRUTH of mathematical patterns. They were looking for truth "out there" in the greatest of all realities. Later, Plato speculated that mathematics pointed to a world "out there," a world beyond the observable, a world of pure mathematical forms. For the Pythagoreans and Plato, mathematics took human minds beyond the constraints of their individual idiosyncratic experiences of the here and now. Mathematical personality was advancing.

The context-driven fundamentals of the early Egyptians and Babylonians focused on angles and devices for measuring length, width, and so on (Posamentier, 2020). The Pythagoreans added context-driven fundamentals that included relationships and incidental properties of geometric figures such as harmony and string vibration. More abstract, but still problem-focused, Plato treated a slave boy's ability to prove a geometrical truth as evidence that the mind could recognize transcendental perfection of forms beyond personal experience of the immediately present world. (Gray, 2008, p. 440).

By the sixteenth and seventeenth centuries, context-driven fundamentals in mathematics expanded significantly. For example, the calculus put in reach the possibility of describing aspects of the world previously thought inaccessible since they required attention to infinitesimals (Alexander, 2014). The calculus was subsequently taught in the context of learning to do physics (Erwig, 2017; Berlinski, 1995). Furthermore, analytic geometry was added to plane geometry and became a required study for anyone interested in physical science. And still there was more.

In the seventeenth and eighteenth centuries an interest in risk, insurance, decisions under conditions of uncertainty, and gambling opened a demand for other context-driven mathematical fundamentals. These demands were largely fulfilled through the probability equations of Blaise Pascal, Thomas Bayes, and the Bernoullis (Diaconis & Skyrms, 2018). Making better judgments under conditions of uncertainty required context-driven fundamentals never before dreamed of by Pythagoras, Plato, or even Newton and Leibniz (Ellenberg, 2014). Here mathematics sheds its primitive beginnings and is robust with a discipline-specific personality all its own.

When contexts shift, some context-driven mathematical fundamentals may prove to be applicable in newly evolved contexts. For example, in the nineteenth century those schooled in the probability calculus of seventeenth- and eighteenth-century thinkers described gases as no one before even imagined (Diaconis & Skyrms, 2018, pp. 165–66). In addition, probabilistic insights led to Carl Gauss's construction of the *normal* (bell-shaped) *curve*. This so-called normal distribution led to speculation in the social, biological, and educational sciences never before imagined (Gigerenzer, 2002; Su, 2020).

By the nineteenth and twentieth centuries, mathematicians began to debate the very foundations of arithmetic itself. Mathematics had become so unique and so evolved that it merited a sort of deep dive into its adult personality!

Abstraction in its purest form became common among professional mathematicians as much as abstraction had previously driven theology from historical tales to accounts of metaphysical possibilities (Pearl & Mackenzie, 2018, ch. 2). Unsolvable problems, proof theory, number theory, transfinite sets, Hilbertian Hotels, and halting algorithms all became focal points for understanding math well beyond any immediate utility (Fortnow, 2013).

Understanding math required looking beyond calculation and toward foundational reasoning (Lockhart, 2017). It became unavoidable to make the psychological distinction in serious contemplation of mathematical reality between true understanding and mere belief in the application of a set of protocols (Chinn & Samarapungavan, 2011).

The idea that training in calculation alone could suffice for comprehensive math education waned. Students taught calculation were increasingly told there was more to consider in the nature of mathematical thinking, especially in more advanced math studies (Hacker, 2016). Psychology and eventually neurology were revealing more evidence that mathematical understanding went beyond the cultural phenomena of: "See, do this as I do it" (Dehaene, 2011; Lyons & Beilock, 2011). Being "good at math," even being "very good at math," was hinting at something more advanced, namely, mathematical heroism.

THRESHOLD CONCEPTS

The move from calculative training toward imaginative engineering and abstract constructions requires that math education realign itself with new pedagogical ideals. These ideals include new paths for some select heroes whose personalities so align with the personality of mature mathematics that intellectual space must be prepared and pedagogical prompts utilized in place of "See this? Do this as I do it," and for that reason we should downplay standardized tests, which merely confirm that effective mimicking has taken place. A curricular and instruction path must be created that invites students who are potential heroes to experience deeper visions into mathematical passion.

Ideals that honor wonderment, adventure, courage, respect for unequivocal truth, and zeal in the shared and sustained search for truth must be part of that path in the curriculum of those who are very good at math and especially those few who are capable of becoming the future heroes of math.

Imagine an educational format; call it "the Great Conversation of Humankind" (Wagner et al., 2018). In this format, curious and open-minded investigation into every claim to know is valued more than rote representation of facts or ability to mimic protocols. But to participate in the Great Conversation, students have to be prepared to autonomously exercise reflective thinking.

Thresholds are abundant, each with demonstrable markers, so educators can recognize when mere training should give way to independent investigation. Thresholds mark the line between teaching students basic context-driven fundamentals and clearing the path for them to think along the lines of mathematical personality. This path gives them a chance to discover if their own personality development fruitfully fits with the flourishing personality of math itself.

Illustrations and demonstrations of the utility of context-driven mathematical tools and strategies are necessary preludes to thresholds; however, these preludes are inadequate for completing a sound education in mathematics for those who are very good at math and with the potential for heroism.

Thresholds bring students into a whole new way of thinking about and thinking within the evolving mathematical superstructure (Harris, 2015). Thresholds mark the transition for students from ritualized signaling to the beginning of autonomous speculation about further utilities and foundational constructions. For example, having a student observe and then count, say, six green balls, as a manipulative makes sense as an early introduction to the practice of counting. But such manipulatives show no reason why people count as they do; it shows only that this sort of performance is done this way (Sosa, 2011; Wittgenstein, 1975). Manipulatives, demonstrations, and illustrations are generally indoctrinative practices of ritualized signaling.

Thresholds mark a moment of passage from ritualized signaling to reflective mathematical thinking. For example, more advanced learners entering the Great Conversation may be drawn toward a threshold by a teacher prompting reflection on the concept of "six green balls." A teacher can note that "six" is in an adjectival position in an English expression "six green balls," but that does not make six a property of any single ball. Could six be a property of a set, a teacher might ask?

The teacher then might proceed, explaining, "All depends on what is meant by the term 'set' doesn't it?" This could be occasioned by introducing preliminary thinking about the concept of sets (Gopnik & Graf, 1988; Perkins et al., 1993). And there is still more in this threshold moment.

In the example above, "green," in contrast to "six," is an adjective predicating a property of the balls. "Six" may predicate membership in a properly constructed set, but it is clearly not a property of any ball. In contrast "green" is a material property of each ball. As thresholds are approached, students can grow in reflective contemplation, whereas with an indoctrinative strategy, such as teaching simple counting, no further contemplation is evoked. Counting is a gateway practice directing student attention toward mathematical functions. It leads toward thresholds, but never through them. Thresholds benchmark teachable moments, moving learners from ritualized signaling to reflective discernment.

On the other side of any threshold, learning goes beyond mere mimicry of calculation and, for some, can reach lofty levels of abstraction (Wagner, 1982, p. 79). Passage through thresholds leads always to some further meta-understanding of what it means to "do mathematics" (Wagner, 2006, p. 36–37).

Learning *to do* mathematics means learning the value of avoiding contradiction, it means learning the value of genuinely settled proof. It means learning there are problems that have enticed mathematicians for centuries (Maor, 1991). It means learning why foundational matters in mathematics are philosophically important (Mankiewicz, 2000). It means considering reasons why mathematical techniques are subordinated to scientific investigations at times, even though the mathematics looks as though it would lead scientists elsewhere (Adkins, 2004; Wittgenstein, 1975).

When all goes well, doctrinal obedience and propensity to recognize answers on multiple-choice items should give way to openness and wonder (Rowlands, 2014). When thresholds are missed, doctrinal obedience overruns mathematics education and its commitment to truth-seeking.

Excessive indoctrination is usually the cause of missed attention to thresholds. Consider, for example, that there are college students who learn to calculate probabilistic equations but fail to understand statistical applications in a physical world (Smith, 2014). For them, finishing a problem provides little in the way of evidence that they have acquired understanding either of the nature of probability or of its utility in problem spaces beyond a contrived calculational competency. When thresholds are missed, participation in the Great Conversation of Humankind remains beyond reach in mathematics education. Passage *through* thresholds is where true disciplinary understanding begins (D'Agostino, 2020).

MATHEMATICS EDUCATION TODAY

Context-driven fundamentals such as counting, addition, subtraction, multiplying, division, equational arrangements, and so on are warranted material for indoctrination in ritualized signaling today, just as in antiquity. Today, however, researchers recognize that mathematical *understanding* depends on neurological capacity (such as parietal lobe efficiency) as well as several culturally derived abilities early training can afford (Gopnik, Meltzkoff, & Kuhl, 1999; Levitin, 2014; Secolsky et al., 2016). A focus on understanding recognizes math as more than a set of tricks and gimmicks, but also as a mental adventure.

Imagine, for example, that students could reasonably conclude on empirical grounds that adding one drop of mercury to one drop of mercury counts as a refutation of the arithmetical fact that $1 + 1 = 2$. They might conclude reasonably, that $1 + 1$ only sometimes equals 2 and other times $1 + 1 = 1$! Or again, they may be reasonably troubled by the impression that nature is not bound by arithmetic any more than arithmetic is bound by nature. So, why study arithmetic? The facts of arithmetic must be seen for what they are. But what exactly are they?

Certainly, arithmetic originated with ritualized signaling—and human brains naturally responsive to such signaling (Lockhart, 2017). But eventually, arithmetical facts appeared to extend beyond ritualized signaling.

Arithmetical operations, for example, coordinate human instincts for aggregating the results of various performances and observations.

To many people even today, mathematics is doctrinal, much like catechism study for the religiously minded (Graham & Kantor, 2009). If these people become math teachers, their instructional strategies may approximate ritualized, algorithmic procedures for loading student minds, much like programmers who load algorithms into computers. However, the production of right answers to standardized test items does not exhaust the goal of purposeful mathematics instruction in the contemporary world.

To have students become well-versed in apt ritualistic signaling may have been sufficient in antiquity, and even today may serve well in managing checkbooks and cash registers. But math learners today who are unable to review critically or speculate into quantitative claims about opinion polls, epidemiological distributions of health and disease, reports from financial markets, or charts and graphs representing quantitative data—just to name a few items—are at a serious disadvantage to others who can do those things. These learners are neither very good at math nor for all practical purposes even good at math regardless of test proficiency. Modern societies are compromised to the extent that the citizenry is unable to be given new understandings of math.

Teaching strategies in the template of ritualized signaling practices was sufficient for antiquity, but math instruction is fossilized when all that matters is replication of specific protocols for calculating correct answers (Aczel, 2015; Kjeldsen et al., 2014).

Teaching students the Pythagorean theorem is an example of a context-driven fundamental. Students are routinely told that in the case of right triangles with "a" and "b" representing the sides of the right angle and "c" the hypotenuse, then $a^2 + b^2 = c^2$. Teachers may imagine they are demonstrating for students a proof of the theorem by showing them a right triangle, measuring its sides that show a = 3 and b = 4 and surprise! Square each and add them together and the sum is twenty-five. In a flash, all students recognize that the square root of twenty-five (something they were previously indoctrinated to believe) is five.

"There you have it," the unimaginative teacher declares, "proof that the theorem works!" The alleged "proof" sits there inert. In fact, it is not a proof, but it is rather an illustration of properties contingent upon the axioms of plane geometry.

The creative teacher recognizes the dangers of excessive indoctrination in this ritualized signaling approach to teaching Pythagoras's theorem. Teaching of the theorem can be an opportunity to initiate learner reflection on the whole idea of mathematical truth—a threshold experience. The teacher can display an overhead in which the sides of the right triangle are equal, that is, a = b. The teacher can then suggest that "a" and "b" each be assigned a length of 1. Now what happens?

One squared is one. One squared plus one squared is two. The square root of two is an irrational number. It looks like it should go on endlessly well beyond 1.414. . . . But how infinitesimally close could ever be close enough to the "real" square root? The answer is that any finite number squared will not be two. This sort of imaginative challenge is aimed to overcome the risk of excessively indoctrinative, ritualized signaling, and instead to prompt independent critical thinking.

Mathematical *understanding* involves at least some feel for the creative employment of mathematical strategies and intuitions. It involves knowing how and when to size things up mathematically (Soni & Goodman, 2017, pp. 171–72). Like other forms of understanding, mathematical understanding is exhibited through innovative applications or novel strategies successfully engaging *a problem space*. A problem space is successfully engaged when understanding effectively frames the problem and then employs probing strategies, revealing more of the previously unknown.

Matthew Cobb (2020) paraphrases neuroscientist David Marr's definition of problem space nicely as follows:

> First, the problem to be solved has to be stated logically; this theoretical approach frames how the problem is explored experimentally or is modelled. Second the way the input and the output of the system are represented has to be determined, along with a description of an algorithm that could get the system from one state to another. Finally, it has to be explained how the level could be implemented. (pp. 276–78)

A vivid example identifying problem space for secondary school students' imagination is the engineering challenge of the Apollo 13 spacecraft. This challenge was dramatized in Ron Howard's film *Apollo 13,* based on a memoir coauthored by Jim Lovell, one of the astronauts. There was a malfunction in the oxygen system of the Apollo 13 lunar re-entry capsule. The command vessel and the lunar re-entry unit had different shaped oxygenation capsules. One was cylindrical and the other box-shaped. Oxygen was available on the command ship, but there was no way of getting the oxygen there into the lunar vessel prior to re-entry. This and the other materials in the astronauts' spacecraft defined the largely geometrical problem space.

Engineers on the ground figured a way to create the now famous "mail box" construction. Engineers at NASA in Houston created a prototype. Using materials available to the astronauts, engineers showed them exactly what to do. The engineers were imaginative and abstract in their thinking. Now their instructions to the astronauts had to be indoctrinative: "See, do this as I do" was essentially the command. No time for further speculation. This is warranted indoctrination. Do it now and do it this way. But in coming up with the solution, the Houston engineers were very good at math and exhibited their understanding in the "mail box" creation.

INDOCTRINATION: BENCHMARKING, A DANGEROUS GOOD

Freedom from indoctrination results in freedom to doubt. Education should count as a success when students become capable of productive doubting. The capacity to share doubts and recommend adventuresome hypotheses is fundamental to education (Wagner et al., 2018). Indoctrination should never be so extensive as to eliminate individual inclination to speculate. In short, *doubting is what rescues people from intellectual complacency.* Rescue from intellectual complacency is critical to the advancement of mathematical understanding.

Thresholds are successfully transitioned when learners express well-reasoned doubt about knowledge claims within a discipline. Then they are not intellectually complacent. *Doubt benchmarks that a successful passage through a threshold has been executed.*

Knowledge is inside human minds (Byers, 2007). It is often propositional or algorithmic, and in either case is necessarily less shareable than an ideal such as the ambition for truth. Knowledge is what we share when we look to the utility of warranted belief claims. Knowledge is about apprehending approximate or "true enough" conclusions. Knowledge is individuated among cooperating persons. Person A knows things that person B does not, and vice versa. But the ideal of truth cannot be meaningfully limited to any one person and is shareable through participation in the Great Conversation (Wagner, 2011, pp. 404–5).

Truth, not knowledge, is the ideal that accommodates human big-braininess (Lakoff & Nunez, 2000). Other animals and computers have legitimate claims to knowledge capacities, but only humans express the ideal of truth-seeking. As Jordan Ellenberg writes, "The measure of our success is whether what we do enables people to understand and think more clearly and efficiently about mathematics" (Ellenberg, 2021, p. 149).

The elusive point of every science and of mathematics itself is to push beyond the context-driven fundamentals beyond the thresholds, and then, beyond the thresholds, the search for truth bootstraps its way to ever better explanations of the world (Heard, 2019; Mazur, 2016, pp. 68–69).

Indoctrination compromises the intellectual foundation upon which theories and clever experiments can properly be built (Csibra & Gergely, 2006).

In the end, two things matter when it comes to understanding the pedagogical significance of indoctrination versus warranted indoctrination in mathematics education. First, educators must benchmark when indoctrinating practices are warranted because of learner ignorance of fundamentals. Second, educators need to recognize when indoctrination is unwarranted and blocks learner advancement toward the next appropriate threshold. Understanding indoctrination benchmarks for educators involves both understanding when indoctrinating practices are necessary and when ritualistic signaling practices begin to block the path forward.

When unwarranted indoctrination continues unabated, new paths for student understanding are thwarted. Students who are merely good at math are not likely to advance to becoming very good at math. Students who are very good at math will be challenged even to imagine a path to mathematical heroism. The personality of math is hidden in the mix of unwarranted indoctrination.

There are moral consequences, too. For example, respect for the moral agency of the student as an independent thinker is endangered when instruction short-circuits advancement through the next threshold of understanding. This short-circuiting places at risk the student taking his or her rightful place in the Great Conversation of Humankind (Wagner, 1986; Wagner & Dede, 1983).

Before summarizing, consider a threshold experience for advanced learners in secondary school or beyond through the following dialogue.

Teacher: If there were an infinite number of universes, what are the chances that there is one exactly like our own?

Student: Exactly like our own?

Teacher: Yes.

Student: I guess it would be certain if there were an infinite number of universes.

Teacher: I see. What are the chances that there would be two universes exactly like our own?

Student: I don't know. That is really unlikely.

Teacher: Take a guess.

Student: That would be certain too?

Teacher: Why?

Student: If the universe has an infinite number of universes, why not two?

Teacher: What are the chances an infinite universe could have an infinite number of universes exactly like our own?

Here the teacher has just opened the gateway to contemplation about the consequences of concepts like infinity (Deutsch, 2011). There is no indoctrination here, warranted or otherwise. The passage through the threshold reveals abundant grounds for wonder, speculation, and reasoned evaluation of the mathematical world never dreamed of prior to the threshold passage (Cook, 2020; Stewart, 2013: Strogatz, 2019). Here the student is in the world of the Great Conversation of Humankind.

In antiquity, students were indoctrinated in pictogram depiction and then in learning to count (Massey, 2002). Ever since, students have been indoctrinated into appropriate fundamentals of a discipline or field of study prior to and as a part of developing any skills of independent, disciplinary investigation (Nehm, Kim, & Sheppard, 2009).

This recognition of the limited—but core—value of indoctrinating practices leads to the following concern. It is a gross illusion to suggest that either curriculum or teaching strategies can be designed in a sterile fashion, free from all moral consequence. Teachers do more than instruct. They should do much more than prepare students for the next standardized test. They should strive always to move as many students as possible through thresholds of understanding in a respectful and open-minded search for previously undiscovered truths.

Passage through a threshold is benchmarked by evidence that learners are able and inclined *to express well-grounded doubt* about knowledge claims in various areas of math. To repeat from above, such doubt is what rescues learners from intellectual complacency. More than any other sort of evidence, it is the expression of reasoned doubt that benchmarks successful passage through a threshold. When the threshold has been successfully breached, further indoctrination is no longer warranted. Learners are finally engaged in the Great Conversation of Humankind just as they should be, and some are on their way to becoming heroes of mathematics.

KEY IDEAS OF CHAPTER 1

1. *Indoctrination* is warranted but only to the extent that it brings students to the threshold of novel thinking within and about math.
2. *Number sense* is a product of evolutionary development.
3. *Numerical representation* is a context-driven fundamental.
4. *Abstraction* in its purest form became common as interests in unsolvable problems, proof theory, number theory, halting algorithms, and more evolved in the wake of continually advancing skills of calculation.

5. *Thresholds* are demonstrable markers indicating student passage beyond basic fundamentals at one level to realized opportunities for inquiry at more advanced levels.
6. Learning to *do mathematics* is more than increased calculation skills.
7. Mathematical *understanding* is what makes calculation matter.
8. *Doubting is what rescues people from intellectual complacency.* Rescue from intellectual complacency is critical in the advance of mathematical understanding.

Chapter 2

The Personality of Math

THE EMBRYONIC UNFOLDING OF MATH

Aristotle divided the world between substance and properties. Personality is a special type of property. A personality becomes a personality through interaction with other personalities. No man is an island, and neither does a personality unfold in isolation. This is true for human personality, the personality of other animals, and, analogously, it seems true of the personality of academic disciplines. Each academic discipline has its own content, borders, and substance. And as with animals, all these are affected by encounter with other disciplines. In the sciences, math is universally interactive with all the other sciences.

Imagine a zygote. The zygote receives nutrients from a nurturing mist each day. The zygote has an inherent structure, but without engagement with other forces there would never be any readout on what that inherent structure might be.

Humans create subject matter as humans create zygotes. In neither case do humans write the code for what is inherent within the creations, but without human engagement neither subject matters nor zygotes would come to be and unfold their distinctive interactive personalities.

Adults often ask children what their favorite subject is. Here the argument is that this question is closely akin to asking them who their best friend is or their favorite movie star or television character. The question is about the evident personality they respond to in the subject matter, friend, or fictional character.

Apt teaching should lead students to a relatively well-defined sense of a subject matter's personality. This will certainly involve teaching students presumptive facts of the discipline along with increasingly potent inferential practices within the subject matter. This may be likened to a kind of indoctrination, but more is needed. Mastering a discipline means *getting a feel for it* as well. This means sensing its mysteries, the sorts of achievements it honors, and the deeper philosophical thinking it stirs up.

Teachers of many subject matters such as history or literature put the personality of their subject matter into especially high relief in the world of their students, but this may not be so true for the physical sciences and mathematics. For too many students, math is the one subject that is not seen to have a personality, but rather it is just boring or it is an ugly nuisance. Consequently, after many students graduate, whenever they encounter mathematics, it confronts them with an unwelcome challenge rather than an old friend to engage. Why is that?

For many people any encounter with math was simply imposed upon them. Outside of a math class itself, math is too often treated as just a troublesome tool to manage in order to get something more important done. In short, for many graduates, math is a roadblock on the way to things that matter and never something that matters in and of itself.

Since math is so central to the renewed emphasis on STEM studies, math needs to become more personable to students. It must become more than a treacherous list of recipes and algorithms; it must become something more than what computers do best. These days students do not even have much need to learn simple arithmetic for tracking their checking and credit accounts since with the right software purchase, all they need to do is enter numbers and read results from time to time. Instruction in that software can be accomplished in a day or so.

The purpose of this little book is to sketch for teachers some of the personality of math, and then to explain how this personality can be revealed effectively to students. This illumination of personality in math lessons over time has great potential for making math as welcome and intriguing to many students as any other discipline.

Math has a very uncommon, mysterious quality. This mysteriousness is not a matter of merely being difficult to understand or formidable in the number of recalcitrant problems that confuse and sometimes defeat the energies of early students. In fact, math can be quite open and transparent. Often it is this very transparency that leads to haunting questions, questions unlike those of any other discipline. The very fact that math has truths that emerge across cultures and that are unequivocally true makes it stand alone among all disciplines.

Think about it. Neither history nor literature has so much agreement about unequivocal truths across cultures (Bradley & Howell, 2011). And while physics, for example, is cross-cultural, it continues to adjust some of its most basic theoretical foundations. What is true in these areas is certainly true in all other academic disciplines—well, all except math.

Thousands of years ago, math was "discovered" in several cultures and in several ways. These cultures were unknown to one another, but like the zygote developing into a fetus and then into a person, math developed in ways that came to be recognized as the same subject across geographic and historic borders. Is math hard-wired in the human species, and the cross-cultural discoveries genetic and neurological in character? Is math the functional structure of some computational matrix? These questions cannot be answered here, but what is important is that only in math are such abstract speculations about origins tantalizingly irresistible.

The idea that math has a personality is not new. In the dialogue *Meno*, Plato's character Socrates shows that a slave boy could be prompted to figure out a geometric truth about triangles in general. Plato believed there was a world of pure ideas where all human intellects once awakened could look and take part. In his famous allegory of the cave from the *Republic*, Plato suggests there is excitement for those who look past immediate experience to the light of eternal truths. But Plato thought most people look only into a world of shadows. In their conversation with others about the shadows, if they agree, they take this as sufficient for construction of true understanding.

Agreeing on shadows is not unlike the experience of many students attempting to master what seem like the illusory contrivances of mathematics, things serving solely to make the dominating voices of cave life (teachers and examiners) happy. If this constitutes their experience of an impoverished personality, then math for these students is tedious, if not altogether absent. If math has any content for them at all, it must be dark and gloomy, something at best endured as little as possible.

Darkness and gloom need not be inevitable in the study of math. In fact, darkness and gloom and a world of shadows is nothing like the personality of math, certainly not its personality as embraced by lovers of math such as Plato, Euclid, and the Pythagoreans. For lovers of math, from ancient Mayan cultures to the Middle East, India, and China, math was celebrated as a light of illuminating truth. In these cultures, math facilitated trade and hence social interaction. In these ancient cultures, math opened the heavens to exploration by creating strategies for charting the heavens and figuring out the return of the seasons. Math dispenses with shadows and frees people from imposed intellectual habits, the chains of Plato's metaphorical cave.

Today, one of the things binding people to the shadows might be the tyranny of standardized test preparation. Math is an instance of Plato's light dispensing with the mere shadows on cave walls. Math frees people from the whimsy and capriciousness of self and others. Math is not confining, any more than traffic rules of the road are confining. Traffic rules make it possible for people to proceed more efficiently than they would if roads were left a lawless free-for-all. And, just as there are generally reasonable rules for making road travel more efficient, the axioms and proven theorems of math extend its utility to other sciences and cultures, establishing something of an intellectual permanency not experienced anywhere else in life.

In addition to math's ability to organize thought with increasing transparency, its accessibility to proof gives reason to accept its evolving transparencies. Proof and utility, both prominent features of math, have been part and parcel of math for more than two millennia. This has led to much speculation about the mathematical mind. Is it one locked into a search for Platonic truth, or is it one carved by genetics and evolution which graces only a few (Hadamard, 1945)?

This dichotomy alone is admittedly odd since it suggests a mixture of metaphysics, neurology, evolution, and culture to approach a reasonable answer. Other disciplines draw no attention to metaphysics. But to many mathematicians even today, the study of pure math is an other-worldly pursuit. As an example of this mindset, one of the authors had a calculus teacher who avowed in class one day that the reason he loved math so much was that its truths would remain true even if the entire physical universe were to disappear.

The iconic mathematician Grigori Perelman has turned down the Fields Medal and a million-dollar prize for his work in mathematics, including solving a conjecture from the French mathematician Henri Poincaré. Perelman said in effect that he did not deserve any prizes since he invented nothing. The truth was there all along and he just happened to be the first to find it. He has an almost religious reverence for the study of math and what those who study it should respect about their study. Dr. Perelman said Dr. Richard Hamilton, a mathematician who did earlier work on the problem, deserved as much credit as he did, Interfax reported. "To put it short," he said, "the main reason is my disagreement with the organized mathematical community. I don't like their decisions; I consider them unjust" (*New York Times*, July 1, 2010).

Remember too, math is still relatively young in human intellectual adventures, extending a previously evolved number sense shared in part with many other mammals. Art, music, and language all predate math. While notched counting sticks and other devices go back tens of thousands of years, the earliest mathematical documents from Babylonia date back merely to 1750 BCE (Lakoff & Nunez, 2000). Of course, after math appears, it affects nearly everything: art, music, language, trade, the sciences, and so on.

Beginning near Plato's time (428–27 to 348–47 BCE), proof became the backbone of mathematical exceptionalism. Proof turns much of what is deemed to be true through practice, experience, and intuition into universally reliable foundations upon which to build while watching the majesty of mathematical construction unfold (Mazur, 2005).

EUCLID

There are too many great mathematicians from days of antiquity to mention in this brief sketch of math's personality. But one person who is often cited as the greatest of all mathematicians will be discussed (Mazur, 2005; Bell, 1957; Boyer, 1959).

Euclid (ca. 365 to 300 BCE) recognized the transparency of truth in math and wanted to share that potency of math so all could appreciate its splendor. By axiomatizing mathematics, Euclid gave a transparent understanding to theorems such as the Pythagorean theorem, which had been around in different cultures for millennia but which had never been given a solid basis. In his *Elements*, Euclid also showed possible incongruities between the concepts of length and number. In that same book he showed appreciation for irrational numbers and infinity, concepts most mathematicians at that time tried to avoid.

Providing a model for mathematics ever since, Euclid started with a handful of the simplest and most intuitive propositions as axioms for a beginning, and then he laid out transparent conclusions justified one step at a time. For example, take two of the simplest geometric objects one can imagine, namely, points and lines. In *plane* geometry, one and only one line can be drawn between two points. Simple enough. But now what if one contemplates the defined line a bit further?

Is there any reason to believe the line must end at the two points or might it extend beyond? If the line can extend beyond the two points how far can it be extended? Are there limits? What if thinking about the line goes in another direction, namely into the interior of the line? Is there any reason to imagine a line must have width? Is the line segment between the two points divisible? How many times can the line segment be divided in half? Could any and all internal segments be determined by an infinitesimal numbering indicator?

It is mysteries such as these that lure lovers of math into her embrace. Many people competently employ line drawing as part of a plan for building a structure. But to someone who intuits it, there is a subject matter at hand beyond the skillful employment of a mechanical process. Herein lie hints of the discipline's haunting personality. In this case, a student today, much like an ancient Greek mathematician, can ponder not just the use of a representative line segment but can also contemplate universal characteristics of "lineness." In both cases, the result is that the imagination is drawn into contemplating infinity.

INFINITY

Everyone today thinks he or she knows about infinity. Infinity goes on forever. There is no last greatest number above which there is no other—right? And do not forget about the infinitely small! There is no line that cannot be divided, again and again, an infinite number of times. That too is right—is it not?

Students today are told canned answers to both the questions above. But canned answers especially in this context tend to mask rather than reveal the alluring nature of mathematics. It is figuring out what such answers mean and what are the consequences of those meanings that reveals the mysterious, intriguing, and yet optimally reliable personality of math. The personality of math is optimally reliable because, despite so much mystery and intrigue, each new insight—once proven—can be forever depended upon. Questions about the infinitely large and infinitely small were investigated twenty-five hundred years ago. Progress has been made, but so much is still unknown and may even be unknowable. Math's personality is always inviting but never wholly transparent.

SOME REALLY BIG STUFF

Imagine the very biggest number you can imagine, and call it n. Can you add one more to it? Of course, that is just $n + 1$. Now rather than add one, is there any reason you cannot add that whole number to itself, $n + n$, making it twice as large? Of course, that works too.

Here things get tricky. Can you imagine an infinite number? Pretend you can imagine an infinite number. Give it a name. For convenience, call it "Tory." If Tory is an infinitely big number, can you still add one to it? If not, why not? If you can, then explain how that would work. (Pause: please answer these questions to yourself before proceeding.)

If Tory is infinitely large and you can add one to it, what does that do to the idea that Tory is infinitely large? If Tory plus one is bigger than Tory, then does it not seem that Tory must not be infinitely large. Is that the way you see it?

What makes a number infinitely large? If Tory is an infinitely large number, can you add a second Tory to the first Tory? Can you multiply an infinitely large number by two? If you can multiply an infinitely large number by two, can you multiply an infinitely large number by another infinitely large number? Are you getting confused?

Here math is seen as being more than calculations with black-and-white answers at every turn. Perhaps math is not quite as straightforward as you once thought! The questions above reveal mysteries that have tantalized math's best friends for centuries, indeed, millennia. Using line segments in ancient Greece to plan the construction of a temple or today to plan a garden behind a house is a far cry from contemplating properties of lines that lead unavoidably to questions about the nature of infinity.

HILBERT'S HOTEL

David Hilbert was a lover of math. Thinking about the infinitely large, he imagined what might happen when two infinite sets might seem to collide with one another. Must one set be truly bigger than another? Must such a collision prove one set is truly not infinite and must on reflection turn out to be bounded and contained within the other?

Hilbert has an exercise for you to consider if you truly want to find something of the personality of math. Imagine a hotel with infinitely many rooms. A convention of an infinite number of guests comes to the hotel and fills up every room. So far so good. I bet you can imagine this scenario easily. So, what happens when a late conventioneer shows up?

You may well ask, who dreams this stuff up? Mathematicians do. They can be a fun group of people imagining things no one has ever seen portrayed on television or anywhere else. Mathematicians love math and have fun teasing her with new tickles, hoping to reveal more of her mystery. Math has nooks and crannies inviting those who become her lovers and heroes.

So, here we are at Hilbert's Hotel and a newly arrived conventioneer needs a room. The hotel is filled. So, what to do? The two sets seem equal in size and are evenly matched. Is this not like saying for every odd natural number there is an even natural number and so the two sets are the same size?

Are you getting a bit disturbed by all this? This is like having a romantic interest in another who makes ambivalent remarks from time to time. The remarks may seem impossible to disentangle. Yet you keep trying because there seems to be a glimmer of hope that you might succeed.

Here is how Hilbert figured things out. Send an attendant to the first room and tell the guest there that he or she must move to the room next door. Invite the new conventioneer to move into the room as soon as it is ready. Go to the second room and tell the original guest to move to the third room because the guest from the first room is moving in. Continue this process *without end*. All is well. Still a bit confused? One thing to recognize here is the paradox that the statements "there is a guest for every room" and "no more guests can be accommodated" are not equivalent when there are infinitely many rooms.

Remember you already know in any infinite set you can always add to whatever total you may have reached. And, remember that names for infinite numbers are not like names for other numbers. The name for one hundred is, one hundred. You may also call one hundred the square of 10 or the sum of 99 + 1, but in each and every case the name means the same, the number 100. The names for infinite numbers like Tory are more like names for a generating process of sorts, a continuing function.

There is always one more room in the Hilbert Hotel and there can always be one more conventioneer added (Cook, 2020, pp. 12–24). The mathematical concept of the infinitely large has many questions lurking about for those who are becoming patient truth-seekers. This little tour of math's personality is just beginning. That math has intrigue and mysteries to discover should already be evident.

ZENO'S PARADOX OF ACHILLES AND THE TORTOISE

As early as the Greeks worried about the infinitely large, they worried too about the infinitely small. Consider, for example, a paradox imagined by Zeno (450 BCE). The great warrior-athlete Achilles is set to race a lumbering great tortoise. Because of the obvious difference in talent, the tortoise is given a head start over Achilles. Imagine the tortoise's head start is ten yards and the finish line is a hundred yards away. Zeno points out that, once the race starts, Achilles cuts the distance between himself and the tortoise in half almost immediately as the tortoise inches along. But now things appear to get confusing.

To catch up to the tortoise Achilles must traverse half the remaining distance. So far so good right? Yet to cut the remaining distance in half Achilles must advance half that distance in real time. And to get to half that distance, Achilles must cut that distance in half. In fact, since the distance remaining between Achilles and the tortoise can be halved an infinite number of times, it seems that Achilles can never catch up to or pass the tortoise (Mazur, 2005, pp. 140–41)!

Certainly, our experience suggests something different happens with competitors in footraces. Some seem to pass others in real time. Is Zeno under some illusion? Is the logic of infinity he explores an illusion, or is our experience an illusion?

Imagine a news broadcaster today who wants to make a name for himself. He knows of Zeno's paradox. He also counts heavily on the wisdom of personal experience. He does not want logic to confuse what he knows from experience. So, he climbs to the top of the Sears Tower in Chicago. Cell phone in hand, he starts recording a video selfie. He jumps from the tower and after falling for a while he announces: "Fifty stories so far and no problems. I feel fine and all is well."

Is his experience sufficient to show that at the end of the fall all will be as well as it is fifty stories down from the top? Might it be the case his experience is about to change and be accompanied by horrific consequences his previous experience of the first fifty floors could not speak to? Is he looking into the darkness of the cave wall when he should have turned to the light of logic and truth? What if he had known about Zeno's paradox? Could that have made a difference? If the broadcaster bought wholeheartedly into Zeno's paradox, then does it appear he might have made the same jump?

After all, the distance from the top of the Sears Tower to the ground below can be bisected an infinite number of times, so he can suppose that he will never arrive at the bottom. Indeed, Zeno's paradox reversed might show the broadcaster never quite left the top of the Sears tower except by some infinitesimal amount that can always be further divided. To fall any distance, the broadcaster must first fall half that distance.

And to fall that distance, he must first fall halfway of that. And so it goes. The tiniest distance can always be halved again. This infinity of halving the distance would cause an observer below to conclude the broadcaster never jumped. Any descent would be too small to notice and growing smaller by half each infinite sliver of a second.

Most people can ignore infinitely large numbers. No one will be staying at the Hilbert Hotel, and no one will ever travel to the ends of an infinitely large universe. Cosmologists today wrestle with infinitely large numbers from time to time, but they are a small and uncommon group. On the other hand, scientists from antiquity onward have been bedeviled by notions of the infinitely small. The idea that space or time can be infinitely divided led to exasperation among many scientists about what constitutes the smallest fragments of reality.

CALCULUS AND THE INFINITELY SMALL

Even the creators of the calculus, Isaac Newton and Gottfried Leibniz, were challenged by the idea of an infinitely small (Alexander, 2014). In one way or another each pondered, as did many of their predecessors, if matter or all of reality might be constituted of tiny particles called *infinitesimals* (Alexander, 2014, pp. 212–13). If so, how small must these particles be? The concern is that, if no such particles exist, then there is no substantive foundation for the world and all is an illusion. Here are echoes of Plato's cave. Does math have the power to turn away from the shadowy illusions of the darkness, or does math itself keep us in the dark?

There simply is no mere calculation to solve such problems. Yet the calculus leads to exacting approximations far better than anything previously considered, and the calculus and its offshoots remain today most valued tools of researchers in nearly every scientific or engineering field.

Galileo said all of science should be mathematized (Frenkel, 2013, p. 2). But it was Newton's calculus that made it possible to formulate Newton's laws of motion and his theory of gravity. Through these achievements Newton showed how math can give stability and resilience to the sciences over time. The calculus still does all these things and plays a fundamental role in computer science and artificial intelligence. The calculus may not by itself reveal the light of Plato's world of ideas, but it certainly brought light into the cave, illuminating much that previously lurked in the shadows for centuries.

Not to get too far ahead of the unfolding theme of this book, note that math led people to seek truth extending so far beyond appearance that it somehow seemed tied into a supernatural world of its own or at least something beyond this world of sensation. With the calculus, math shed light on much of the world that humans dealt with, clumsily at best. Math showed that much that previously seemed supernatural in essence was evident in the natural world all along. But it took mathematicians creating and employing tools such as calculus to unveil the structure of reality.

As grand as the calculus is, it did not shed light on all the shadows of the world or further mysteries still lurking inside math herself. Newton himself tried to employ considerations arrived at in the development of the calculus to make more rigorous his theological writings, which constituted two-thirds of all his written work (Iliffe, 2017, pp. 85–86).

Even a master of math such as Newton is not yet prepared to look into the full light of mathematics with all its promise and allure. He stood on the shoulders of giants and saw more than anyone into the physical laws of motion, astrophysics, and math, but it only prompted more speculation within him about the real and mysterious nature of it all.

Of course, mysteries continue to surround infinity. But a little mystery never separated lovers—just the opposite. Time to take a look at the human side of math's personality by looking toward some of her most famous suitors.

Aristotle, Plato, Euclid, Zeno, Newton, and Leibniz are mentioned here simply to turn attention away from those whose experience of math has always been to look into the moving shadows on the wall of a daunting cave. We hope to turn heads away from the shadows enough to see some light revealing math as different and more real than perhaps previously appreciated. The moral of the story is that, in order to introduce students to the personality of math, those who teach need to have grasped something of that personality first.

DISCIPLINES HAVE PERSONALITIES

In the chapters ahead, the mathematics at times may become a bit more challenging. More challenging than infinity?

Not much can be more challenging than infinitesimals and infinity. But there may be a few more intricacies in math beyond mere history that will challenge you, perhaps more than the gloss of topics above. To really appreciate math and the arguments presented for math having a personality, it is imperative to share a bit more math technicality so you can appreciate the subtleties of personality. You will even find an equation or two. You will not have to learn to work the equations to continue. There are references cited for you to follow up on if you are interested in a particular moment in math.

The equations, when they appear, are road signs, more to signal curves ahead or a steep hill than to make you "very good at math." These technical road signs are there to remind you this is math we are introducing, with its own personality. We are not just talking about it from afar. To get a grip on any person or any discipline's personality, it simply is necessary to get beyond the simplest gloss from afar. So, be prepared.

In the meantime, here is a short exercise to help you further think about the personality of a discipline as well as about the personalities of those who are heroes of the discipline. Think of a couple of standard subject matter disciplines with a long history of development. Let's say history and physics. You may be good at one of these yourself and maybe even very good at one or the other. So, take a moment and write down three to five characteristics of people who have achieved heroic distinction in history, and then in physics. Do the characters you listed look different, one from the other?

Probably not, and that is no surprise. The people who are passionate achievers about such traditional characteristics are likely to share a number of personality traits in common. Now imagine there is something of a disciplinary personality analogous to the personalities humans evolve over time. List three to five characteristics of what you imagine might be the personality of history and then of physics. Look at your two lists. Does it seem that there is a predictable pairing between the discipline's personality and many of the personalities of its most heroic lovers?

The above was probably something of an easy challenge for most of you. But it is not as common for people to size up math similarly, even though math has surely been around as long or longer than each of the other two. People just do not think often about the personalities of mathematicians, nor of math having any personality at all. For most people, what goes on at the highest levels of math is akin to a secret sect. In what we have started and in what follows, we hope to open the door to the personality of math. And we want to reveal that there are distinctions between being "good at math," being "very good at math," and being an actual champion of math, fully aligned in personality and intellectual depth with the personality features of math itself.

And so next we turn to explore the human side of mathematical personality and the uniqueness of mathematical genius.

KEY IDEAS OF CHAPTER 2

1. *Apt teaching* should lead students to a relatively well-defined sense of a subject matter's personality.
2. *Love* applauds mystery, and math reveals mystery and affection to those who learn to love it.
3. *Beauty* is revealed in the range of number types and in its emerging functions and operations.
4. *Wait, what . . . ?* Experiencing the personality of mathematics involves an experiential *feel* for investigation into the mathematical wilderness.
5. There is more to *mathematical understanding* than being *good at* calculation or even *very good at it*.

Chapter 3

The Human Side of Mathematical Personality

THE UNIQUENESS OF MATHEMATICAL GENIUS

Subject matter disciplines whether in the humanities, the sciences, or even mathematics are always to some extent a reflection of the people who excel and lead within the development of the disciplines. So, who are the folks who excel at and lead math?

A reflexive reaction may lead one to recollect standout students in K–12 education who excelled on standardized tests. To understand students who reflect and exhibit the personality of mathematics, the first thing to do is get beyond looking only at the mass of students who are simply good at math.

When thinking about mathematically precocious children, it is tempting to look at the enormous amount of research in education depicting those who are seemingly above average in math (Marie-Pascale, 2005). This massive literature is invaluable to practicing educators, but it tells us little about the type of people who embrace the world of mathematics so fully that they reflect and exhibit something of the discipline's personality.

The majority of K–12 students who calculate well are said to be "good at math." Those students often tend to be better students in general. This is not always the case. A substantial minority of students who exhibit considerable mathematical competence then eschew interest in nonmathematical subjects, and they neglect the nonmathematical at the expense of those other subjects. But, on the whole, *being good at math* in K–12 is too general a descriptor for identifying students who are destined to truly embrace and reflect the personality of mathematics.

"GOOD AT MATH" IS NOT GOOD ENOUGH: MATHEMATICAL HEROES ARE ADVENTURERS INTO THE MATHEMATICAL WILDERNESSES

At the college level the people majoring in engineering, economics, and the physical sciences employ much math. Typically, these people use mathematics expertly, but they show little interest in seeking deeper secrets of mathematics. This is true even for many undergraduate math majors as well. In contrast, consider two champions in contemporary applied mathematics: Claude Shannon, the father of information theory, and Patrick Suppes, the father of computer-assisted instruction.

Shannon had a knack for looking at aspects of the world from noise on telephone lines to roulette wheel tendencies and imagining a way to use math to model the organizational patterns that held diverse phenomena together. He saw that binary mathematical operations are information. He saw how binary redundancy could preserve information economically. He ventured into the mathematical wilderness proposing that redundancy of information could minimize interference in electrical communication.

Shannon was always mathematizing the world surrounding him. He did math on napkins and note pads when math insights into the natural world occurred to him (Soni & Goodman, 2017). He saw in math a model for mastering natural processes by relying on and then controlling information transfer. Math could be said to be the language of universal intelligence.

Similarly, Patrick Suppes demonstrated great competence in the application of mathematics in research methodology and in designing computer architecture for managing information. Sitting in on his graduate seminar one semester, one of the authors, Paul Wagner, witnessed professors from other areas at Stanford, from physics to psychology, attending the seminar in order to ask Suppes questions about equations that might better serve their disciplinary needs. Suppes believed chance was built into nature, and probability could identify nature's most sustainable trends. When asked a question, Suppes would put his cigar to his mouth, think a bit, and then go to the blackboard and write out a set of equations with full explanation.

Suppes was irresistibly drawn to seeing in math the grounding tendencies of natural reality (Suppes, 1970). The world itself was probabilistic. Algorithms were key to expert knowledge systems for artificial intelligence. Algorithms could achieve reliability of evaluation, but not to the point of subordinating all natural processes to mathematical laws.

In their respective achievements both Shannon and Suppes excelled in applied math as few others. Shannon, the engineer, could rewrite much of reality in mathematical terms like few others have ever done. Suppes, the philosopher, saw reality reflected in the language of math. And he saw in math the best organizational structure for thinking about the probabilistic world. Both heroes of math confronted big questions of applied math far beyond calculation. Neither drifted into contemplation of pure math and number theory, but each saw there was more to math than the technical skills of mastering calculations. Shannon saw math revealing nature, and Suppes saw math demonstrating the indeterminate structure of the world.

There are savants who amaze with their ability to calculate, but that skill rarely leads to the kind of expert applications like those of Shannon and Suppes. A very, very few do calculate beyond comparison and also manage to do theory as well. Take, for example, John von Neumann. Von Neumann was known for his speed of calculation. He amused people at cocktail parties with his speed of calculation, and he took delight in solving math problems faster than the computers he helped design.

But his love and understanding of the personality of math took him well beyond calculation wizardry. With Oscar Morgenstern, von Neumann founded game theory, mathematizing the give and take of human social engagements and suggesting a family of models for extending understanding of evolution. He was also an imaginative designer of computer architecture. In addition, from March 1955 to February 1957 he was the chair of the Atomic Energy Commission (Helms, 1980).

Savant skills of calculation are neurologically interesting, but they are not revealing of Olympian contribution to the development of math, either pure or applied. The personality of math is not revealed through the calculation abilities of savants nor even through the identification of neurological pathways through the parietal or other regions of a human brain (Nieder & Dehaene, 2009). Those who venture into exceptional applications or who articulate novel insights into areas such as analysis, topology, and number theory are few in number.

Noted Stanford mathematician Keith Devlin (2017) offers insight into the concept of the mathematical hero when he comments:

> I came to see mathematics not as a collection of disjointed techniques, procedures and tricks, but as a single, coherent whole, a vast, cognitive landscape, built up over three millennia by some of the smartest people the world has ever seen. It was a landscape that was both rich and beautiful. (p. 4)

Devlin is one of many researchers who are studying the psychology and neurology of mathematical thinking, but, as Devlin admits, those who excel far beyond others who are merely "good at math" are a singularly unique and generally inaccessible subject of study. Consider a paradigmatic hero of pure math such as the Indian mathematical genius, Ramanujan. He was never a particularly good student in general, nor was he known for his skills of calculation. In his elementary years it is unlikely anyone would have speculated he might be like Carl Gauss in any way.

Yet, as Ramanujan advanced into his middle to later teens, he lost interest in any other study but math. He began, he says, having visions of theorems, and he constructed his own notational system for his theorems. He had no other choice since he had not sufficient education even in math to familiarize himself with conventional systems of notation. In his early twenties he sent some of his work to the internationally famous G. H. Hardy. Hardy got mail routinely from people who imagined they had contrived some new mathematical insight, and Hardy very nearly set Ramanujan's work aside when it dawned on him that the notational system corresponded to conventional notational insights. Upon reading through the text, Hardy recognized Ramanujan's theorems as the work of genius.

Hardy brought Ramanujan to Cambridge University to work with him. Ramanujan produced theorem after theorem, each surprisingly apt but without the needed proof. Hardy and another Cambridge mathematician, Littlewood, worked out the proofs and indeed there were workable proofs for nearly all Ramanujan's theorems. But where did such math insight come from?

Ramanujan claimed that in his sleep they came to him as dreams from the Hindu God, Vishnu. Whether from Vishnu or some other source, Ramanujan was consumed by his mathematical adventures. He and math fused together, the human personality married to the discipline's personality, even to the point of the hero seeing his adventure as divinely inspired.

Other than biographies and histories, there are no revealing empirical studies of mathematical heroes like Ramanujan or Hardy. As Devlin said, mathematical heroes are some of the smartest people who ever lived. But they are too few, and they are too spread out over the centuries for the kind of empirical studies typically done on those who are "good at math" and who are accessible to current researchers (Rusconi et al., 2005). This lack of neurological studies on mathematical heroes is simply unavoidable.

And, if neuroscientists investigate neurological operations rather than psychological propensities, it is unlikely that they will get subjects such as Grigori Perelman, Paul Erdös, Maryam Mirzakhani, Akshay Venkatesh, or any other recent superstars of mathematics to allow neuroscientists to distract them from their math work. So, neuroscientists have little hope—at least in the near future—for finding correlations, much less causal relations, in the brains of comparable hero mathematicians (Schwarzlose, 2021).

The great Einstein donated his brain to science. After the first few years it was traded among university offices as a curiosity, a collector's item, but it held no obvious secrets into his genius. So, the absence of study into true mathematical genius is no stain on the record of empirical researchers. It is a consequence of the fact that the information that might be revealing is inaccessible.

Not all is lost, however. There have been some glimmers of insight. For example, we know that savants immediately see quantity without counting, and this immediate seeing circumvents the processing of most people when asked to count, say, a pile of matchsticks. Moreover, some tribal societies see small number collections and spatial distancing without any of the exhaustive mathematical languages of technical societies. PET scans and such have allowed researcher to see that there are visual pathways and activity of the parietal lobe in most people's mathematical counting and number estimation, but those findings explain nothing about the celebrated few who become absorbed in the mathematical personality.

So, seeing small rough quantities and comparisons between large and small is neurologically evident in humans generally and many other animals as well, but becoming absorbed in math's personality is far more than the savant-like seeing quantities by simply seeing countable sums.

Typically, the ability to calculate quickly is distinct from mathematical precociousness. Calculational savants rarely become exemplars of mathematical personality. For example, Ramanujan had an uncanny ability to fabricate theorems that, upon reflection, other mathematicians such as Hardy, Littlewood, and Russell were able to prove. The theorems were provable, although Ramanujan was slow to utilize the tools of proof to justify his theorems. He presented the Cambridge mathematicians with amazing theorems seemingly constructed out of whole cloth, yet he was never known for his amazing speed of calculation or for his diligence in methodically constructing proofs.

On the other hand, he did routinely notice properties of numbers. He once took a taxi and became fascinated with all the properties of the taxi number—or so goes one story (Stewart, 2017, p. 228). He lived within the personality of math and felt no need to deconstruct his images for purposes of practical utility (i.e., by publishing a proof). He found in math that which only the lovers of the discipline's personality can appreciate. He loved discovery in the math wilderness with no other concerns but to find his way about in math's vast domains.

AND OTHER HEROES . . . ?

Euclid is often described by historians as the greatest of all mathematicians. Other historians extend the metaphorical language to designate Carl Gauss the "prince of mathematics." Gauss lived a long life, doing extraordinary work until the very end of his life. Certainly, a long life of mathematical accomplishment makes one's work more visible to history, as was the case with Paul Erdös, Leonhard Euler, and Benoit Mandelbrot.

Gauss, however, was especially unique. He, like the later Ramanujan, saw properties on individual numbers, but Gauss was equally inclined to immerse himself in every aspect of the personality of math, its features, its unexpected applications—he did it all! As an elementary school–age child, he was able to keep the books for his father's business in double-accounting entry. At sixteen, he created a non-Euclidian geometry in which he treated Euclid's fifth axiom about parallel lines as a theorem to be proved and not as an axiom itself (Aczel, 2011).

This geometric theorizing led Gauss (as it did Lobachevsky and Riemann somewhat later) to develop an inclusive geometry extending beyond Euclid's plane geometry. In non-Euclidian geometry, lines become geodesics, and triangles have more or less than a sum of 180 degrees in their angles, but never 180 degrees itself. The geometry of curved space eventually led others to the intrigues of multidimensional modern topology. And Gauss did applied math as an adult, giving the world the standard distribution of error now named in his honor, the Gaussian (bell-shaped) curve.

Somewhat like Gauss, John von Neumann, the twentieth-century mathematician, was savant-like in his ability to calculate, but also like Gauss he was enamored with the theory of math behind the obvious tools of applicability. People like Gauss and von Neumann are rare even among the champions of math in general for their demonstrable skill and enthusiasm cutting through so many sectors of the mathematical wilderness. Most importantly, they shared with the number theorist Ramanujan and others noted above an insatiable love and affinity for mathematical adventure. For each of them a life well-lived was lived in the thralls of adventure in the vast conceptual wilderness of math—an inviting trek most others are deliberately sure to avoid.

So here is a modest step forward in understanding the heroes of mathematics in the absence of a neurological or other refined research strategy. A characteristic feature of every hero of mathematics is being thrilled as much as any adventurer when penetrating an unfamiliar wilderness. As Oxford mathematician Marcus Du Sautoy explains, mathematical heroes are like mountain climbers who want to take on the most challenging climbs imaginable. The goal is not simply to get to the top for the view, but to exercise their skill as they struggle up the ascent (Du Sautoy, 2021, p. 128).

This is unfamiliar and perhaps even intimidating to most others, including those whose tests say that they are "good at math." The heroes of math share together in the personality of math. For math education to truly nurture young math explorers, attention must be given to the students' *sense of adventure* in mathematical exploration and not simply to relentless demands that they do only this particular math now and in only this particular way. Math educators need to learn to become more intellectually tolerant.

Math educators need to careful about imposing on students the alleged "one and only way" to think about math as outlined in some curricular package. One excellent way for math educators to advance their tolerance for a potential prodigy's speculations is to ask themselves: What would cause me to change my mind about the efficacy of the rubric I am imposing on this math student at this time?

As noted above, there are few clues known about the mindset of those who absorb and embrace the mathematical personality. But there are a few. For example, Dehaene (1997) suggests a simple exercise hinting at mathematical precociousness beyond mere efficiency of calculation. Dehaene asked subjects what is two-thirds of three-fifths. Most people run an algorithm in their minds to identify the answer. In contrast, a few subjects, respond instantaneously: two-fifths! When asked how this minority arrived at the answer, they do not report calculating anything. Instead, they report just seeing the answer! They say simply, two-thirds of any three equal parts of entity is two of the three parts!

A more legendary case of someone living within the mathematical personality is Nobel Laureate in Physics Richard Feynman. Feynman tells of being in high school and solving a proof differently from how he was being taught. His teacher gave him an "F" for not "correctly" showing how he got the answer. Fortunately, Feynman's father took his son's paper to a noted mathematician at Columbia University and asked the senior mathematician's opinion of Richard's work. The mathematician described the work as genius for one so young. Feynman opines that he saw things differently from others who were "good at math" (Feynman, 1985). Feynman's father asked the professor to write a note to Richard's teacher about Feynman's solution. The professor did. As expected, the teacher changed Feynman's grade to a well-deserved "A." The point is that what counts as "good at math" in K–12 may not be especially informative about who will be the shapers of the discipline one day.

Stanislas Dehaene and others (Nieder, 2020, pp. 231–233) are trying to detect the neural operations of such math prodigies. Despite modest advances, researchers seem limited to saying little more than that prodigies see the world of mathematics differently from many of the rest of us (Dehaene, 1997). Studies of animal number sense and anthropological accounts of number development among peoples abound, but none of that tells anything about the majesty of what Plato described as the truth of an other-worldly place of ideal mathematical constructs. The personality of math is not revealed by connectionist models of neurological pathways nor studies of widespread mathematical utility among peoples and even other animals.

In K–12, being "good at math" may be about little more than doing well on standardized tests when compared with other students. Unfortunately, there is no compelling evidence that such comparisons accurately characterize champions and lovers of the discipline's personality. We know the champions and lovers of mathematical personality by their deeds, but all that is after the fact. As of now we have no way of identifying who will merge with the personality of mathematics nor how educators might bring those who may be simply good at math into a more intimate relationship with the personality of math.

IS THERE MORE TO MATH THAN SIMPLY BEING "VERY GOOD AT IT"?

Could those who are *very good at math* at the college level comprise a better study set for identifying traits of the human personality commensurate with the personality of math itself? Not likely. Most accounts of mathematical genius indicate that the merging of human and discipline-specific personalities occurs prior to students' late teens. There are outlier examples such as the forty-year-old lawyer George Boole's development of an algebra still used for constructing computing languages, but Boole's achievement places him in the tail of any Gaussian distribution curve of mathematical heroes.

Unfortunately, in the twenty-first century with its massive industrial-like approaches to schooling, being "very good at math" identifies little more than students majoring in subjects requiring substantial, but otherwise conventional, math knowledge of one sort or another. For example, students going into finance or accounting might be seen, by friends at least, as especially skilled at math. In physics and various areas of engineering, topology and conventions of analysis may dominate.

These are all challenging fields of mathematics, but when employed merely for their utility in well-defined problem frames they give little hint to what it means to venture into the mathematical wilderness for fun or out of irresistible habit. Nonetheless, the math required for degrees in finance, accounting, or even engineering and most sciences does not typically lead one to becoming a mathematical hero.

Again, the example of Gauss is informative. As noted above, he helped keep his father's business accounts while a mere child. But this alone gave no hint of his future as a champion within math's personality. Fictionalized accounts in the media do little to illuminate the traits of those who find fulfillment and success through induction into the personality of math. They may even distract from the search for matching human personality profiles with a personality profile of math wherein a "marriage made in heaven" can be realized.

The psychologist of optimal experience Mihaly Csikszentmihalyi describes something he calls "flow." An optimal experience is one in which sense of self dissipates in the all-consuming task of exercising one's excellencies in undertaking a challenge (Csikszentmihalyi, 1988). When experiencing "flow" a person loses a sense of self, merging with the quest for excellence in the task at hand (Csikszentmihalyi, 1990). Imagine extending the experience of flow as something akin to a self-fulfilling obsession extending beyond a challenge of the moment to a marriage of sorts, one bringing the personality of the investigator into alignment with the personality of the discipline.

For example, think of the television show *Young Sheldon*. Sheldon is portrayed in one episode as doing his father's taxes at ten years of age. The bookkeeping and calculating talent for such purposes is regimented and differs greatly from utilizing math for opening new vistas into reality. There is little insight to be gained from seeing the idiosyncratic Sheldon master such calculative abilities.

But Sheldon does so much more. He looks for mathematical accounts of nearly everything in the physical world. He ponders deeply, but a television show cannot capture the mind of genius pondering the unknown with mathematical agility. Sheldon's commitment to math is characterized as idiosyncratic weirdness. The writers of the sitcom may think they are portraying the nature of bright young physicists and mathematicians to be, but none of this reveals the hero's loss of a sense of self during the relentless pursuit of new paths through a deep and haunting wilderness. It is not surprising that a leading mathematician of today, Marcus du Sautoy, should describe champions of math as heroes and their life as akin to a wilderness journey (Du Sautoy, 2021, p. 6).

Hollywood has also portrayed Nobel Laureate John Nash, Stephen Hawking, and Alan Turing in equally naïve and misleading ways. Hollywood stories always break down to social intrigue and struggle, and the endpoint of accomplishment pops into view at the crest of social success. When the writers tell of these heroes, the viewer cannot help but get the feeling that all is akin to the same story as the trite and easily anticipated plot: boy meets girl, boy loses girl, but boy wins girl in the end. The turmoil and toil of pushing past mathematical fascination to progress through its wilderness are never ably captured.

KNOWING MATH IS NOT THE SAME AS BEING A MATHEMATICAL ADVENTURER

Students in every area of engineering need to know math—a lot of math. In the middle of the previous century, they may have been teased about walking about with their slide rule and their devotion to trigonometry. But how many became star architects of mathematical disciplines? Not many. How many Claude Shannons (Nahin, 2012) have you heard of? Add students of computer science, logic, economics, physics, population genetics, and even mathematics itself; how many college grads with those degrees become distinct paradigms of a mathematical hero—applied, pure, or both?

Most mathematically competent graduates in the disciplines and professions above use mathematics in a variety of ways to get things done. They may even exhibit considerable novelty at times in how they creatively employ mathematics. Mostly, however, they carefully rein in mathematics for the purpose of creating shortcuts (Du Sautoy's term) rather than give full bridle to its development. So, turn now to graduate schools. Again, more often than not, in medicine, law, epidemiology, economics, the other social sciences, and perhaps even in the sciences at large, graduates utilize math but seldom fall in love with it and develop it further.

The movers and shapers of math in the next generation are most likely to come, albeit few in number, from philosophy (logic), computer science (again, logic), physics, electrical engineering, and, of course, pure and applied math departments. Records from the Graduate Record Exam indicate that folks entering Ph.D. programs in both pure and applied math represent the highest total scores in the aggregate of quantification, analysis, and verbal abilities respectively. In short, math Ph.D.s include a lot of generally very smart people, and yet only a few stand out as paradigms, capable of embracing math far beyond that of fellow graduates.

With relatively few jobs in academia for mathematicians, Ph.D. graduates hire out their mental wares to Wall Street and to the military/industrial complex in general. Some may even wind up teaching in high schools. Remember that Einstein, with Ph.D. in hand, began as a patent clerk. Yet few of these extraordinarily smart people, at least by most standard benchmarks, become paradigmatic equivalents of an Einstein, whether or not they work in an intense math environment. For the most part they spend their time working on the "low hanging fruit," as Du Sautoy opines (2021, p. 265). So where next to turn to find those who exhibit the human contribution to math's disciplinary personality?

To find those who contribute substantively to the personality of math requires some cherry-picking strategies by interested investigators. These cherry-picking strategies must obviously begin with the great mathematicians of historic stature: Plato, Euclid, Pythagoras (if he truly existed), Anaxagoras, William of Ockham, al-Khwarzimi (along with a number of others from the Middle East and India), Blaise Pascal, Fermat, Leibniz, Newton, De Morgan, Boole, Descartes, Euler, Galois, Fibonacci, Venn, Russell, Cantor, Hilbert, Kolmogorov, Gauss, Poincaré, and others leading into the twenty-first century.

This rest of this chapter takes a brief look at several of the historically great figures of mathematics. The next chapter will discuss some of the more recent heroic mathematicians of the twentieth and twenty-first centuries. They are discussed separately since they play the most immediate role in shaping the human contribution to math's personality today.

THE PERSONALITIES OF THE HEROES AND THEIR MARRIAGE WITH MATH

There are entire books written about each and every one of the historically great mathematicians listed above, and there are many others who are deserving, but the point to be made about traits of heroic mathematicians can be made sufficiently by considering a few as paradigmatic. There are wonderfully written and authoritative master volumes such as Bell's *Men of Mathematics* (1957) and numerous books by Ian Stewart and others (Brooks, 2021). With a sentence or two about representative heroes of math to the nineteenth century, the goal here is simply to say enough to reveal an alignment between personalities of math champions and the unfolding personality of math, which distinguishes the field from the personality of other subjects such as history, medicine, engineering, biology, and so on.

Du Sautoy mentions one such characteristic in passing, but it is critical from the point of view of this text. Most mathematicians, he says, "believe there is no point even publishing a proof only 99 percent complete because that last 1 percent can be deadly" (2021, p. 72). Du Sautoy thinks mathematicians ought to lighten up a bit and not be so obsessed with perfectionism. Du Sautoy is focused on utility and misses the point that the obsession is not with perfectionism, but rather with an unrelenting commitment to honesty. *Honesty is fundamental to the personality of math as in no other discipline,* and it may be just as fundamental to the champions of math who neither fudge nor care to promote an idea they honestly have not thought through.

Consider the story of Hypatia, who is alleged to be the first great female mathematician. She lived in Alexandra, Egypt, and was admired by both the public and scholars for her intellectual prowess. In the early days of the Common Era, Christians were persecuted in Alexandria. As fate would have it, a couple of Christians were accused of some heinous crime they could not in fact have done. A mob wanted to exact its pound of flesh by punishing the Christians for their alleged misdeed. The accused turned to Hypatia to defend them. Hypatia was not Christian, but she was trusted as a person with a staunch commitment to honesty. She also knew the accused could not have been guilty of this particular crime. She agreed to take up their cause and spoke in their behalf.

The mob was incensed that she, not a Christian herself, might get these Christians off the hook. They became so incensed that they grabbed Hypatia, beat her, dragged her body through the streets of Alexandria behind a chariot, and then burned her body. Hypatia honored the truth as any true mathematician must. She sacrificed her life for the truth. This is key to the life of a paradigmatic mathematical champion.

Politicians aim to persuade, often by any means possible, and people with goods to sell or grants to secure may be inclined to be less than obsessed with truth. The mathematician aims solely at mastering the quest for truth; near truth is not good enough. Even in probability theory the goal is to get the mathematics right. The goal of the statistician is not so pure. Like engineers, statisticians must have an eye to best bets to address a problem framed with some urgency in the here and now. In contrast, truth is foundational in the personality of math from antiquity onward.

Since Euclid is so often described as the G.O.A.T. of mathematics, it is useful to single him out for description among all the notable mathematicians of Greece and the Hellenic world. Math was developing in India, China, Egypt, and among the Mayans, but nowhere was there a set of individuals attempting to be mathematicians as opposed to being clever people using arithmetical and geometric strategies for getting something done in an applied discipline.

In this early Hellenic flowering of mathematical speculation, commitment to abstract validations of truth abounded. In contrast, the great astronomers of China, Babylon, and elsewhere in the world saw math as a bookkeeping tool for their observations (Berlinski, 2011). *Only the Greeks began thinking of math as a world unto itself* (Hadamard, 1945). Even Plato's student, the empirically minded Aristotle, saw math as an independent subject all to itself (Davis & Hersh, 1981).

Euclid's focus on proof anticipates the dedication to truth referred to above in the life of Hypatia. Euclid saw in math a path to certainty. Other Greek mathematicians, such as the Pythagoreans, saw in math a way to prospect for truth both in the real and supernatural world. Truth, and the certainty it enabled, became defining of mathematical excellence. Euclid tried to sum this up for geometry by identifying five propositions as given because of their resistance to any further reducibility. These axioms, along with twenty-seven rules of logic, became the scaffolding for an architecture of geometry for twenty-one hundred years.

And, lest one think that truth changes with times and cultures somewhat willy-nilly, the changes in geometry that emerged in the nineteenth century at the hands of Bolyai, Lobachevsky, and Gauss led, not to a change in Euclid's identification of truth, but rather to a reframing of the extent of geometric configurations beyond Euclid's *plane* geometry. For example, given the axioms of Euclidean geometry it is impossible even to imagine a round square. Things impossible to imagine are not candidates for truth-securing practices such as Euclid inaugurated, and mathematicians in some sense have followed this standard ever since. Non-Euclidean geometries of the modern era changed, not as truth changed, but as Euclid's fifth axiom was removed from the list of axioms while the other four axioms were left in place.

Euclid's work revealed two enduring features of the mathematician's personality as exhibited in those who become her champions. *First, there is a commitment to identifying with certainty and precision the scaffolding architecture of mathematical thinking.* To the heroes of mathematics, it is no bag of useful tricks to be applied in the here and now as engineers may often do. *Second, there is a commitment to show the scaffolding to fellow adventurers aiding all in the quest for further truth.*

With all the historically noteworthy mathematicians of Hellenic times, it would be distracting to try to take each in turn to bolster these claims. But the issue of commitment to truth can be captured dramatically in the thinking of Plato. Plato was well aware that any geometric figure measured contained imperfections attributed to human inaccuracy in measurement. In addition, he was convinced that any human, even an untutored slave boy, could recognize the truth of the properties of right-angle configurations.

That truth existed not in the properties of any drawn triangle, but rather in the properties of the idea of triangle itself. Such properties could never be revealed through sensory observation, but through the purest of thought the ideal form of "triangleness" could be revealed and worldly triangles themselves all demonstrated to be mere imperfect approximations of the real thing; that is, triangleness as an ideal existing in the reality of perfect forms within which truth is certain and never approximate.

Throughout time many mathematicians, including the great Kurt Gödel and today's Grigori Perelman, concede there seems to be a world of mathematical truth apart from the frayed world of human experience. Mathematicians such as these are still called Platonists. So, among mathematical champions there is unrelenting desire to align one's thinking with truth and not to settle for mere approximations. Therefore, in addition to *honesty*, add to the personality of math commitment to *displaying certainty* of mathematical attributes, and *respect for the existence of truth* beyond mere approximation.

Hundreds of years later in countries surrounding what had been the great library of Alexandria, and farther afield in India and in many western monasteries, mathematics continued to evolve and be studied as though it were something of a passage or at least specialist insight into another world of the most pristine ideas. The relation between mathematical truth and truth of diverse religious sorts seemed at times to travel hand in hand.

For example, al-Khwarzimi, the author of "Kitab al jabr w'al-muqabala" after which the term algebra was coined, saw himself as an adventurer of the mathematical world—an ethereal world that existed above the world of lived experience (Rashed, 2009). When Leonardo of Pisa came across a Latin translation hundreds of years later, he revised and modified this early algebra with a view largely to clarifying and enabling business transactions (Khaldun, 1989).

It is not a surprise that a subsequent disciple of al-Khwarzimi nearly three hundred years later, the poet Omar Khayyam, saw algebra pointing beyond the sensory world as well. Plato's idea of math as a special world of ideas continued to be in the forefront then and it still is for many today (Devlin, 2017, pp. 78–80). *So, a fourth element in the personality of mathematics was that it is truth-securing. Contradiction absolutely invalidates a claim to know for those working within the world of mathematical personality.* But what happens when there seems to be incongruities in math rather than demonstrable contradictions?

Zero for a long time appeared to be incongruous. Was it a number or not? And, if not, why not, and, if so, why should it count as a number? Zero added to something makes no difference. Taking zero away from something makes no difference. Multiplying a number by zero destroys the number. Multiply zero by any positive number makes no difference. Yet when applied to the world, having nothing matters! And if negative numbers count, what separates negative numbers from positive numbers on the number line? Number lines seem in recent years to be neurologically established (Seife, 2000).

In India, mathematicians debated for centuries over whether or not zero should count as a number. European cultures often tried to ignore or circumvent theoretical problems associated with any concept of zero (Brooks, 2021, pp. 25–30). There was no confusion in any culture over whether or not an absence of countable things could exist, but there was confusion surrounding whether, in the very real but abstract world of mathematics, zero was a citizen. If zero was a citizen of that world, it had an uncommon stature since many of its properties were unlike that of the other citizens, namely the natural numbers.

In the monasteries, Aristotlian logic fostered but also constrained all argumentation about both the natural and supernatural worlds. The question became how to bring math and theology together through logic. There was a surprising amount of intellectual achievement during the so-called dark ages due to the work of scholastic logicians. Logicians such as Peter Abelard and especially William of Ockham contributed to developing understanding in math (Kneale & Kneale, 1962).

Trade between Europe and the Middle East led to many of the advances from the Persian and Arabic world making their way into Europe. Much of this mathematics served very practical concerns but, from the middle of the first millennia onward, mathematics became increasingly tied into somewhat mystical contrivances about the supernatural.

Leonardo of Pisa, after encountering Hindu-Arabic numerals in Algeria and elsewhere around the Mediterranean and after being impressed by their usefulness in business transactions, reported discovering mathematical patterns in some flower petal arrangements and even in the outer shells of crustaceans. If fact, the more he looked about, the more it looked to him as if nature was arranged according to the pattern of so-called Fibonacci numbers that people just never before noticed (Devlin, 2017). This was yet another discovery of surreal or even a mystical aura surrounding the nature of mathematics at its roots. This hints at a fifth element in the personality of mathematics.

Beyond pure math developments in the second millennium, math continued to advance undeniable utility as well. Practices of navigation, accounting, physical science, and a number of other important matters were made more precise and efficiently calculable. Math was recognized for its potency for identifying and aggregating data. These potencies revealed new worldly insights beyond the content of math itself, such as in the case of Copernicus reconfiguring the image of the celestial neighborhood of earth and Kepler subsequently making sense of astronomer Tycho Brahe's observational data.

Despite its utility, the haunting mystical character of math is ubiquitous throughout its evident personality. To mathematical heroes, pure and applied alike, math was more than a bag of tricks for organizing thought. For example, the issue of *infinitesimals* concerned determining whether one could correctly say that there were infinitely small numbers, numbers smaller than any standard natural number.

Such questions about the infinitesimals enticed and disturbed the mathematically minded from the Greeks of antiquity to the developers of the calculus. Gottfried Leibniz and Isaac Newton were each convinced that the physical universe was mathematically organized bits of reality and that reality constituted all that physically existed. If the two were right, then there ought to be a mathematical story detailing this structure at the level of even the most impenetrably small distances. This seemed to be what any master intelligence would require (Courant & Robbins, 1996).

Leibniz and Newton's great mathematical achievement was to develop independently of one another what is now called calculus (Boyer, 1959). While Galileo and others had already begun using math to illustrate experimental findings, Newton nearly single-handedly mathematized the science of physics. The title of his masterwork, *The Mathematical Principles of Natural Philosophy,* suggests how Newton became one of the three greatest physicists who ever lived, along with Galileo and Einstein. But Newton also was one of a handful of the greatest *mathematicians* who ever lived.

Newton not only figured a way to manage infinitesimals in describing the laws of nature, he also applied math pragmatically in his government office for finance as well as the best of accountants and decision theorists at the time could have imagined. So practical in his applications of math, Newton interestingly wrote more about theology than about any other matter throughout his entire life (Iliffe, 2017). Leibniz too was open to proclaiming math the language of God. So again, the other-worldly absolute truths of a nonphysical world grounded both Leibniz and Newton's understanding of the mathematical wilderness. Hence, the fifth feature of mathematical personality seems apparent. *Mathematics could never be built out of the material of human sensory observation alone.*

The point to be gleaned from this persistent "supernatural" turn is not that math is evidence of anything spiritual, but rather that it is no mere empirical science either. The governing structure of math reigns like no other science (Yau & Nadis, 2019). Math historically has been seen by its most avid devotees as secreting a profoundness of truth found nowhere else. As physicist David Deutsch has said: "That the truth consists of hard-to-vary assertions about reality is the most important fact about the physical world" (Deutsch, 2009). Even theologians who turn to math to bolster a theological position are careful not to bend the rules of math, but, if some sort of gerrymandering is required to bring math and theology together, they usually require theological principles to give way—not those of math (Nirenberg, D. & Nirenberg, R. L., 2021, pp. 256–58).

An interesting case of employing math to bolster a theological claim was sketched by Blaise Pascal. Pascal was a mathematical prodigy. Young Pascal (like Gauss centuries later) kept his father's business records, but soon Pascal's prodigious accomplishments in mathematics beyond accounting had become so well-known that Christian Huygens, whom many proclaimed the greatest scientist of the era, once said that not he but rather young Pascal was the greatest scientist of the century (Posamentier & Spreitzer, 2020, p. 125).

Like Newton, Pascal was both a scientist and a mathematician. Today statisticians, decision theorists, computer scientists (the computer language Pascal was named in Pascal's honor), and psychologists studying decision-making under conditions of uncertainty all have a fondness for referencing Pascal early on in their book-length writings (Devlin, 2008).

In the early modern era, probability theory was emerging as a mathematical tool beyond compare, and Pascal along with Fermat, Laplace, and the

Bernoullis was one of the founders. Probability theory changed how we see the world from actuarial and insurance practices to gambling and astronomy. The role of math in decision-making under conditions of uncertainty is said to begin with Pascal's famous wager.

The story goes that Pascal had a friend who lived a dissipated life of gaming, wine, and women. The friend wanted to know how he could improve his betting odds in games at different levels of play. Pascal helped him, but Pascal then went further and invited this hedonistic atheist to consider the best bet on how to live his life. What you say? A bet on how one should live his life?

Think about it. Each and every day we each make that bet—do we not?

Here is how Pascal proposed the bet. Imagine, he told his friend, that you could live longer than anyone has to date and that your life is filled with the riches of wine, women, and successful gaming. How much pleasure would that amount to? Surely anything can be quantified in at least in a form that can be estimated, so be generous, friend, with the number you give me. But no matter how large the number, it will still be finite.

Now, Pascal proceeds, if you allow what the Church teaches, several consequences follow. First, if God exists and is prone to punishing behavior such as yours, you will suffer an infinite punishment of eternal damnation which you can avoid by behaving in a god-fearing manner. Second, with or without the consequence of eternal punishment looming, the Church claims that working with it and God's plan you will one day be rewarded with an eternity of infinite pleasure. You do not need to see the equation to think that the simple *possibility* of obtaining an infinity of happiness dwarfs any merely finite pleasure!

So, Pascal concludes the best bet is to live as the Church advises, for, if the rewards are far greater than any in this present life, then it is the best bet. Even though there is no certainty of benefit, the amount of reward is so considerable that, if it turns out to be true, it trumps the possible value of any other course of action. It makes sense to bet on a long shot when the possible payoff is very large—eternal bliss—and the risk is losing only a relatively small amount—the sum of finite pleasures of the hedonistic life. This is the turning point, historically speaking, in formalizing decision-making under conditions of uncertainty.

Of course, the fly in the ointment is that a different Church with very different standards might make a different promise. Which should one choose? What if there is a plethora of religions, each touting high-sounding promises for different patterns of behavior, how should one choose among them?

Pascal's work shows that math was so respected that some found it tempting to use it to bolster theological claims. In addition, in Pascal's book *Pensées,* one sees a mind at work seeking profoundness of truth stretching beyond mere physical surroundings (Rogers, 2003). And a century later a pastor, the Reverend Thomas Bayes, constructed a theorem to show that the use of varied prior probabilities for calibrating subsequent belief could lead to many varied probable conclusions under conditions of uncertainty.

In the twentieth century Kurt Gödel, the greatest logician of the century, was still relating math to the theological (Wang, 1996). This does not mean that the two are necessarily related, though the historical record shows similarity in temperament from Plato to Gödel. Perhaps in relating math to the mystical realm, a paradigmatic example can be found in Leonhard Euler's comment describing his discovery of imaginary numbers: "i is real. . . . This seems extraordinary to me" (Stipp, 2017, p. 184). The hint of Platonic heavens for numbers seems never to fully depart from the terrain of the mathematical wilderness.

In the eighteenth century, Maria Gaetana Agnesi became the first woman to publish a book in higher mathematics. She was much influenced by Newton, but, like Newton, she was more preoccupied by religion and math than by physics. Her fame was great and, despite male opposition, Pope Benedict XIV insisted that the University of Bologna offer her a lectureship (Mazzotti, 2015, p. 154). She turned down the lectureship so that she could concentrate on math and a life of prayer. She identified a curve still known in geometry by her name. She was most proud that it was the result of pure analysis of metrical properties and in fact had no immediate application in the world at the time. (Mazzotti, 2015, pp. 157–64). It was purely a monument to her successful trek into the wilderness.

Pascal, Bayes, Newton, Leibniz, Agnesi, and their colleagues were not simply "good at math," meaning proficient at mental calculation. Rather, these heroes set their minds on the search for profound truths, truths which are not simply answers to satisfy an equation or complex algorithmic protocol. Math lures devotees through mystery even more than through the promise of certainty.

Tell fourth graders trying to work with fractions that it is to help them begin an adventure, and it is not just a regimen that if followed keeps the surrounding adults from displaying displeasure or disappointment with their efforts! Learning fractions seldom is presented to students as an approach to a new world of adventure and conjecturing. Yet, it is certainly important for any potential hero of math to appreciate that questions without answers open up the mathematical wilderness, while too often what the math curriculum offers instead are answers without questions.

In the following chapter, we will explore how the trends initiated in this chapter have become more robust in the two hundred years of the present era. The reader will find the allure of the wilderness remains and the sense of adventure required to enter is greater than ever. And, if possible, the density of the wilderness becomes more and not less evident, the challenges steeper, and the climb to the top of a mountain of understanding more satisfying. Humans have invented machines to do the calculating and even to create some simple but novel proofs. Still, the machines depend on humans to outline the paths to be taken, not the other way around.

KEY IDEAS OF CHAPTER 3

1. Like a human being with a distinctive personality, the characteristics of the personality of math place certain requirements on those who would truly get to know it. Five of the most important of these are that the potential friend
   - must be completely *honest* in whatever claims are made,
   - must have respect for the existence of truth beyond approximation, *truth that is exact*,
   - must be committed to displaying *the certainty* that math can achieve, not settling for anything less,
   - must work to display truth by producing *proofs* that survive scrutiny and statements that are *free of contradictions*, and
   - must recognize that, while math is rooted in the common world of counting, often for purposes of trade, and holds inestimable value enabling humans to decipher patterns in visible nature, *math's objects*—squares, prime numbers, and all the rest—*are not built out of the material of human sensory observation alone.*
2. *Champions of math* come in different forms: There are *purists*, *applied*, *crossovers*, and *epistemic* champions. Each thinks far beyond being very good at calculation.
3. *Human number processing* is an active area of scientific investigation. The parietal lobe, for example, seems evident as a necessary pathway for all quantitative thinking. Still, scientists are only beginning to speculate how experiences of courage, love, and persistence constitute the human personality that is so well aligned with the personality of math (analogically and allegorically speaking).
4. *Schooling practices* only teach how to step rightly and prepare for the next standardized test. *Education* aims at far more. Education aims for *understanding*, the sort of understanding that welcomes learners to investigate further into the riches of *intellectual adventure*.
5. In math, *nothing (0) matters more than nothing*. In fact, nothing matters a lot. In math, nothing (0) separates the positive numbers from the negative numbers. By itself zero is neither one nor the other of all the numbers. Zero (what a lay person might call "nothing") all by itself has a unique set of properties that matter as no other number does. In

math, even zero is more than nothing, but it is different from all other numerical somethings and certainly not nothing—as they might say in the children's book *Alice in Wonderland*. Ordinary people never worried about nothing (0). But, mathematicians argued about it in India and the Middle East for over five hundred years. Those whose personality align with the personality of math can understand. Others, perhaps not . . .

6. *Calculation*: computers and humans both calculate, but *humans can also do math*.

Chapter 4

Two Takes on Recent History

Pure vs. Applied Mathematicians and Women in Mathematics

THE TENSION BETWEEN PURE AND APPLIED MATHEMATICIANS

There is an unprecedented population explosion of the human species in progress. The species has passed the seven billion number and continues to grow. Are there predictable limits to such growth? Bee colonies have a number sense that leads them to recognize when a hive has gotten too big, and a young queen leads a group of bees to found a new hive. If they didn't do that, the original hive would die from its own cumbersome inability to work efficiently securing resources for all who are part of the hive (Nieder, 2019, pp. 187–92; Dehaene, Dehaene-Lambertz, & Cohen, 1998).

Mathematicians who use mathematical game theory to model evolution cannot help but speculate if there are limits to how big human communities can grow and still be efficient, or if the entire species can grow itself into a state of universal catastrophe. Centuries ago, Thomas Malthus worried about the latter. Some scientists today have constructed doomsday calculations indicating when Mother Earth may throw up her hands and declare "enough is enough" and rid the planet of the species exhausting all her resources at such a frenetic rate (Poundstone, 2019).

On the other hand, optimists may look to science and math and note that with the rise in population there will be proportional increases in applied mathematical and scientific talent available for solving the pending problems of population growth, climate change, and more. But optimists should be cautioned that at present there are at best only 100,000 research mathematicians serving the urgent needs of nearly seven billion people (Stewart, 2017). And, of course, the number of mathematical heroes within that number, while it is surely greater than at any time in history, is bound to be far less than 100,000.

People use more math than ever before, and the majority of humans living today depend on the expert use of math by trained specialists for their daily survival. Yet research mathematicians are not just trained specialists, and even the budding heroes of math may find it difficult to find employment where their creative talents may flourish. Indeed, many Ph.D.s in mathematics today turn to jobs outside the academic world just to make a living. They are prized for their ability to calculate or construct algorithmic programs for thinking machines, more than for doing the kind of thinking that led to creating thinking machines in the first place.

The heroes of mountaineering relish the challenge of finding their own path up the mountain side. Completing the challenge is the reward, not the view from the summit. Mathematicians understand why many of their colleagues still prefer blackboards to a computer keyboard. Nonmathematicians are not likely to understand such things. Mathematicians work on chalk boards so they can erase and start again and again.

Jessica Wynne is something of a groupie around mathematicians, in addition to being a professor of journalistic photography. In her book, *Do Not Erase: Mathematicians and Their Chalkboards* (Wynne, 2021), she collects autobiographical notes from mathematicians around the world, and they let her take photographs of their office blackboard as well. The autobiographies along with the photographs create a collage for the nonmathematically minded to see something inside the mental workshop of research mathematicians. Their task and their joy is to further mathematical thinking and not simply to calculate a result (Stewart, 2017).

For these mathematicians, it is far more rewarding to ponder the P and Not P problem in machine thinking than it is to plug in a set of numbers to be algorithmically managed and deliver a final calculation (Fortnow, 2013).

In this regard, the queen of the truth-seeking disciplines has changed relatively little since the Babylonians and even less since the Italian Renaissance, when modern mathematics turned toward proof and novel abstract analysis in unprecedented ways. The human side of the discipline's personality has changed no more than the truths of mathematics themselves. It is climbing the mountain that rewards, not the view from the top. Once the summit has been achieved, they look about, but then champion mountaineers and math heroes look for another challenge, finding little solace in staying on the summit too long (Du Sautoy, 2021).

We have seen that looking toward those in school who are "good at math" may tell us little about the human side of the personality of math. Noted

Stanford mathematician Keith Devlin has been unabashed about publicly speaking of his own mathematical deficiencies and early disinterest in math (2000). He is now a theorist of mathematical intelligence, its personality, and its possible neurological correlates. Devlin studies not only higher-level mathematicians, but also those who are truly paradigmatic of the human side of math's personality (Devlin, 2008).

In schools, being "good at math" is largely credited to those who calculate quickly and accurately and to those who obediently and successfully follow specific algorithms for solving problems. Unfortunately, these traits do not often reveal much about math that quickens the heart of those who will become its champions.

As mentioned in the previous chapter, there are idiot savants who calculate extraordinarily well. In "school talk" they may count as "good at math." A much-written-about example is a set of twins who could see a box of kitchen matches dumped on a table before them and name the number of matches almost immediately. They look at the pile, then toward one another, each nods and then one gives the count and the other agrees. When placed in separate rooms they cannot accomplish this feat. No one knows why not. In any case, their talent is calculation (Rubin, 1974), and that is *not* the soul of math

At the beginning of the twentieth century, G. H. Hardy, indisputably one of the greatest number theorists of the past and present centuries, spoke on behalf of many lovers of mathematics when he described fascination with its beauty, elegance, and simplicity. Hardy was such a purist, he spoke uncharitably to the press about one of his own proteges, mathematician extraordinaire, Norbert Wiener. Hardy declared Wiener not a real mathematician because the focus of Wiener's work was to apply math to the world (Hardy, 1967). The world thought of Wiener as a mathematician, but his own mentor, Hardy, did not.

Wiener invented cybernetics, a foundational system in early computer design. During World War II he also designed feedback loops to recalibrate anti-aircraft guns targeting enemy aircraft more proficiently than human marksmanship could ever achieve. Certainly, this all took some pretty serious thinking, imagining how math could be applied in these situations (Ferreiros, 2016). So what if the work is applied—does it not resonate with the creativity and personality features of math? The ancient Greek, Arabic, Indian, Chinese, and Mayan cultures all began with mathematical applications (Richeson, 2019b; Ernest, 2006; Mazur, 2005; Allman, 1976). So what discredits Wiener, a true master of application, in Hardy's eyes?

Despite Hardy's dismissal, Wiener was not just merely clever at calculation. He had seen a world that could be revealed by inventive application of mathematics. That world could be made subordinate to mathematical craftsmanship. Wiener, like Claude Shannon, Alan Turing, and others of this era, saw math deeply as a sort of architecture, one capable of re-structuring the world. These champions of application were not interested in the metaphysics of mathematics. They were not interested in what might be behind mathematical truth. Instead, they were interested in uncovering and then further subordinating the world to formative powers of mathematical structuring (Pearl & Mackenzie, 2018; Poundstone, 2019).

Hardy's dismissal of those who, like Wiener, apply math as not belonging to the heart and soul of math is misguided. (It may be noted that Hardy himself contributed to applied math when he co-authored the Hardy-Weinberg Law still central to the study of population genetics.) Nonetheless, Hardy does draw attention to math's deep resources for metaphysical investigation. If there is unequivocal truth to be found, surely the place to start must be in the metaphysical depths of mathematics. If we can grasp the light of truth rather than remain in the shadows, then turning to the deepest and most metaphysical aspects of math must be the place to start (Hadamard, 1945).

The search for the deepest truths of mathematical foundations must be as revelatory of math's personality as is its extraordinary utility in opening up for human intervention areas of control over the natural world. From physics to genetic drift, from information theory to computational causal analysis, math *empowers* humans in nearly Promethean ways. And it does so while using enduring, cross-cultural, timeless truths. These are two of the most prominent aspects of math's personality, and they are unequaled by any other discipline.

WOMEN IN MATHEMATICS

Since antiquity there have been fewer female than male heroes of mathematics (Osen, 1975; Walker, 2014; Williams, 2018). What to make of this—aside from the fact that historically, many educational opportunities were routinely denied to women?

One of several factors that led Harvard President Larry Summers in 2006 to resign his job after a relatively brief and turbulent stay in office was his opining in 2005 that there may be gender-determinate grounds for evident differences both in mathematical proficiency and in inclination to favor math-heavy studies. Psychologist Camelia Benbow attracted similar ire for her empirical studies which she claimed show inherent gender differences in mathematical proficiency between boys and girls (Benbow & Lubinski, 2007).

And, more recently, Katherine Johnson's book describing her and other African American women's treatment as "calculators" at the Johnson Space Center in Houston showed that these women's talents were minimized until they saved the day by arguing successfully that their calculations for Alan Shepard's *Freedom 7* Mercury capsule to return showed a different path than the male "experts" were committed to implementing (Johnson, Hylick, & Moore, 2021).

Certainly, Johnson's book demonstrates that she and the other "calculators" were subjected to bias and prejudice. And the controversies sparked by Summers and Benbow have led to much arguing for and against their positions. Issues of bias and even prejudice may explain a lot of these sorts of incidents, but they are not relevant to the theme of this book. Why not?

This book is not about being "good at math." This book is not about identifying who might or might not be good at math, nor is it about the reasons and causes of why someone is *good at math* or not. Instead, this book is about the alignment of certain personality traits with what we believe are accommodating analogous "personality" traits of the discipline of math. The contention here is that, regardless of race, gender, religion, or other matters, the personality of math remains stable. And the human personality traits of those who become math heroes are shared among math heroes regardless of social distinctions or advantages of any kind.

We are not neglecting the fact that extraneous factors can prevent people from ever discovering their own math-inclined personality traits or that social factors may prohibit access to mathematical study. These are all factors affecting those who may become identified as "good at math." But this book focuses solely on the idea of those who do develop a mathematical personality aligning with the personality of the math itself. The hope is the outcome of such study may guide educators to look beyond designating students as "good at math" to looking for signals suggestive of capacities which, if developed, could result in the flourishing of heroic mathematical excellence.

The personality traits of mathematics and mathematical heroes mentioned previously are gender-neutral. Indeed, the very first trait mentioned, namely unrelenting commitment to honesty in evaluation, was illustrated in the life of antiquity's first female math hero, Hypatia. Hypatia was certainly subject to bias as women have often been in male-dominated mathematical sectors throughout history (Dzielska, 1996). But social bias does not necessarily dictate the inherent personality traits we discuss.

If Hypatia is an exemplar of a personality trait aligning perfectly with a personality trait of math, then so too is Maria Gaetana Agnesi who, nearly a thousand years later in the eighteenth century, wrote one of the first texts in Europe on algebra. Her text struck the presiding pope, Benedict XIV, as underscoring the other-worldliness of math and thus served as evidence of the other-worldly altogether. The pope intervened on Agnesi's behalf to endorse her for a faculty post at the University of Pisa. Her commitment to math unworldliness is another gender-neutral characteristic of math heroes, as the reader will recall, and it certainly is not something typically associated with either gender (Mazzotti, 2015).

Looking toward the human side of the personality of mathematics, it is clear that relatively little changed over the centuries. Might there have been some whose personality development was compromised by surrounding bias, prejudice, and such?

Of course. But, as far back as the Babylonians, the personality of the heroically minded persons pursuing insight into foreboding mathematical wildernesses required courage and a sense of adventure. This has remained largely unchanged, and has proved as natural to men as to women (Imhausen, 2016). When the Italian Renaissance brought math and reinvigorated interest in Greek geometry, ideas of proof, and novel abstract analysis back to Europe, first to Italy and then to the rest of the European continent, it did not do so explicitly earmarking such in gender-based theorizing. The personality of math and its heroes was reinvigorated, but not especially changed, nor did it become more or less gender- or race-specific in any way (Ernest, 2006).

The unchanging personality of math and the apparent stability of personalities who become lovers and heroes of math has led to fruitful investigation into the mathematical mind (Frenkel, 2013; Berlinski, 2011). No serious research into the mathematical mind suggests any gender or racial relevance. One unique element as alluded to in the previous chapter is the inclination of humans to search for Platonic truth in math. Does such truth exist, and can humans detect evidence of it?

Perhaps the personality of math is carved by genetics and evolution and gracing the minds of only a few (Hadamard, 1945). This possibility suggests a mixture of metaphysics, neurology, evolution, and culture to approach a reasonable answer (Byers, 2007). Other disciplines draw no attention to metaphysics. Yet to many mathematicians, even today, the study of pure math is an other-worldly pursuit most profoundly exemplified in the modern era by the Name-Worshippers of Russia (Graham & Kantor, 2009). But before discussing other mathematicians over the centuries, it is important to note that there are so very few women mathematicians that may be cited. The reader familiar with the "pop" literature of the day may ask, "What about Lord Byron's daughter and compatriot of Charles Babbage, Lady Ada?"

Oddly, Lady Ada, whom many have heard about in a literature written by non-mathematicians, was not accomplished in mathematics. She failed to assist Charles Babbage in writing instructions for coding his proposed thinking machine. Ada did become something of a cult figure in recent years because a couple of literary writers created a mythical version of her that never existed. Lady Ada was actually a lady of leisure, one generally unsuccessful in her every pursuit, including gambling, where she literally lost the family jewels (Holt, 2018, pp. 169–80)! Ada, like many strivers throughout history, was in love with fame, not mathematics. She is not an exemplar of math personality, but she was rather a "groupie", following the exploits those who were. Her life does show one can be intensely fond of math, revere it, and yet not be a champion of it.

There are many extraordinary women mathematicians who deserve attention for mathematical accomplishment and yet get overlooked in all but specialist books and historical surveys of mathematics. These women are lovers of mathematics who illuminate what it means both to love mathematics and to do mathematics. So, before commencing a more historical survey, the reader will perhaps forgive the decision to discuss women in mathematics somewhat apart from the rest of the story.

The botanist and geneticist, Noble Laureate Barbara McClintock, famously insisted that in the sciences a woman's way of knowing is no different from that of a man. Knowledge of reality is knowledge of reality (McClintock, 2012). As applied to math, this is especially so.

Knowledge of math is knowledge of math, and is not the expression of some gender identity. Consequently, the focus in this book is to reveal the genderless personality of mathematics. What we are doing here is neither a history of mathematics nor itself a mathematics book. The point is simply to show that, in the case of women as much as in the case of men, the personality of mathematics has to be exceptionally alluring to the personalities of precocious individuals to secure their commitment to the personality of math.

Women have been discouraged from developing their love of math in part because they were for centuries excluded from higher education. Nonetheless, the robust passion for math is found flourishing in each and every mathematical hero. No one becomes a math hero by accident, nor by mere cultural influence alone (Aczel, 2011).

When historians of mathematics pontificate on who are the greatest mathematicians of all time, three names are always mentioned: Euclid, Euler, and Gauss. Think also of the great names that are mentioned a bit less often: Newton, Leibniz, Pascal, Bayes, the Bernoullis, Hilbert, Fermat, Quetelet, and others! Among the luminaries listed, one seldom hears the name of a woman mathematician. Is that troublesome to you? It should be.

STILL, THE NAGGING QUESTION: WHY NOT MORE WOMEN?

Catherine Chung recently wrote a novel titled *The Tenth Muse*. It is a depiction of what could be a nearly biographical account of a hundred or more noteworthy women mathematicians. Chung depicts a range of reasons that together account for the absence of women's names from the list of great mathematicians. One reason, however, is *not* lack of talent. There have been women of talent whose works are well documented and surely there are many others whose works slid into obscurity, overshadowed often by male mathematicians who replicated the same work (Williams, 2018).

Men overshadowing women's work is not always a result of nefarious intrigue, though that cannot be ruled out in every case. Still, in most cases, a man producing the same results as a woman tends to get the lion's share of credit even if he was a Johnny-come-lately to the theorem, conjecture, hypothesis, or proof. Over time, the male mathematician, out of social habit and expectation, often ends up with all the credit for the discovery.

Sophie Germain was one of the first serious mathematicians to take on the challenge of solving Pierre de Fermat's last theorem. Fermat had asserted that (in modern notation) no three positive integers a, b, and c satisfy the equation $a^n + b^n = c^n$ for any integer value of n greater than 2. The theorem was not solved fully for nearly 350 years, and many mathematicians spent a lifetime devoted to it before American Fields Medalist Andrew Wiles put the finishing touches on its proof in 1994 (Devlin, 2008). But Germain made strides in this direction. She was able to show that for any prime p greater than 2 and less than 100, the equation $x^p + y^p = z^p$ has no solutions when x*y*z is not divisible by p.

Carl Gauss, the aforementioned "prince of mathematics," recognized Sophie's brilliance and possession of all the characteristics for being a premier hero of mathematics. Gauss tried sponsoring her for a doctorate, but prejudice toward her gender was so high that even with Gauss's support, her candidacy as a mathematician could not get her over the hurdle of male prejudice among the rest of the Gottingen faculty. Sophie did have the personality of a mathematician. This personality entailed an unrelenting commitment to aligning with the personality of math itself regardless of the social odds opposing her advancement and acceptance among the ranks of credible mathematicians.

Sophie Germain was followed in the nineteenth century by a Sophia of similar heroic talent. Sofia Kovalevskaya was born in 1850 into a family headed by her father, a Russian general. In addition, her family had many neighbors and friends who were scientists and mathematically literate. Early on Kovalevskaya proved to be a child prodigy. Her family nurtured her talents as they travelled. These travels brought the family into contact with many notable scholars and scientists, such as Charles Darwin and Thomas Huxley' even Dostoevsky was a close family friend. From an early age she had an intense interest in math. Her interest in math grew so intense that by the time she was thirteen her father tried, unsuccessfully as it turned out, to put a stop to it (Kovalevskaya, 1978, p. 6).

Sofia Kovalevskaya wanted to pursue mathematical studies. But she could not officially attend doctoral studies at a Russian university (Posamentier & Spreitzer, 2020, pp. 302–8). However, a Russian woman could do advanced study outside Russia with the permission of her husband. So, she married. She married solely for the purpose of pursuing advanced study in mathematics. The new couple went to Berlin initially, where Sofia hoped to study with the purist Karl Weierstrauss of the Friedrich-Wilhelms-Universität Berlin. She so impressed Weierstrauss that, when the university refused to admit her because she was a woman, he took to tutoring her on his own.

She had to circumvent chauvinism from three universities to become the first-ever woman Ph.D. in math in Europe. Weierstrauss championed her dissertation. He advised her to submit her dissertation as S. Kovalesvsky. Given her record of publications and her dissertation, the University of Göttingen granted her a Ph.D. in 1874. Only then did the university learn it was granting a doctorate in mathematics to a woman.

She did credible work advancing the theory of Newton's challenge to "square the circle," and her imaginative work on the rotation of solid bodies won her the Paris Academy's prestigious Prix Bordin. Her work was used subsequently by mathematical physicists doing work on particles interacting with force fields. As a result of her work, she was granted a chair in the Russian Academy of Sciences and added to the editorial board of *Acta Mathematica*, both firsts for a woman. Perhaps because of facing her own challenges despite indisputable talent, she took time out to write a partly autobiographical novel about women in a man's world and a sketch about a Russian childhood (Berlinski, 2019, pp. 177–83).

Kovalesvsky's greatest discovery was to add to the work of two of history's greatest mathematical heroes: Joseph-Louis Lagrange and Leonhard Euler. In the absence of friction, the total energy of a mechanical system always remains the same. The integral cases for the motion of a rigid body are referred to as "tops." One was called the Euler top. It referred to a rigid body able to withstand torque (external twisting forces). The Lagrange top spins about its axis on a flat horizontal surface with gravity acting vertically. Together these two tops' moments of inertia reveal how much torque is need to accelerate angular momentum about a given axis by a given amount (Richeson, 2019a). Kovalevsky discovered a third top!

Contrary to the expectations of all mathematicians of the day, Kovalevsky pointed out that this third top does not rest on symmetry as did the other two tops. Mathematicians now agree that the three tops exhaust the possibilities for integral systems, and the work on tops was a peak moment in mathematical physics which still holds true today. Here the personalities of three mathematical heroes are evidently in alignment with the common personality of math itself. These heroes loved the adventure, could sustain the challenge of pursuit into the uncertain, and, as Kovalevsky herself reports, felt an attraction for mathematics that was so intense it was impossible to resist.

There you have it! Male or female, it is the intense love of math that leads to an alignment of courageous and adventurous personality sustaining investigations into the mathematical unknown that identifies the heroes of mathematics. It is not culture, race, gender, education, or family that creates the marriage among these personality traits. Such matters may inhibit an individual from discovering their own personality and its natural alignment with math, but in evident mathematical heroism each of these traits are inevitably present.

Young women exposed to the personality of math may find an irresistible pull to overcome local cultural prohibitions against their pursuit and eventual alignment with the personality of mathematics. Now that women are admitted into Ph.D. programs in math and now that there is an emphasis on bringing women into STEM studies, the story of women in mathematics may have a new beginning. This new story might begin best not with the earliest great female mathematician, Hypatia of ancient Greece, but rather with a more recent heroine named Emmy Noether.

The reason to begin the new story of women in mathematics with Emmy Noether is that, when all bias is laid aside and people talk about the world's greatest mathematicians, her name might very well be included along with Euclid, Euler, and Gauss. For example, no less than the great Albert Einstein himself said of Noether's work, "Noether was the most creative mathematical genius thus far produced since the higher education of women began" (Neuenschwander, 2017, pp. 6–7).

What makes Noether so important in a book on the personality of mathematics is that both her work and her life are so paradigmatically distinctive from a faux heroine such as Lady Ada. Despite the current fashionable popularity of Lady Ada, few girls can find a math role model in Lady Ada because they have neither the means nor the temperament to live the life Ada followed (Holt, 2018).

Lady Ada, daughter of Lord Byron, was more attuned to being a socialite, a gambler, and a "groupie" of great intellects. Charles Babbage gave her the one chance she could claim to be an up-and-coming math hero when he allowed her a chance to edit his early notes on coding a thinking machine. She squandered the opportunity, offering Babbage nothing of particular use. In fact, during the time she allegedly was working on the notes, she gambled and lost so much money that her mother literally had to sell the family jewels to bail Ada out debt (Holt, 2018, 169–80).

In contrast, many women, and men too, can find in Noether a life and temperament exhibiting a calling for the love and adventure of mathematics beyond compare. As mentioned throughout this book, the human side of the personality of mathematics does not center on speed and accuracy of calculation (Su, 2020; Wagner, R., 2017). Instead, those who become the champions of mathematics are intrigued either by the tempting search for universal truths governing the foundations of mathematics, or discovering in math how the orderly or near-orderly nature of the universe seems laid out. Noether, like Euclid, Euler, and Gauss, was intrigued by both possibilities.

Noether began doing fundamental work in number theory (Tent, 2008). Her most famous work became indispensable to physicists studying particle physics (Neuenschwander, 2017). And, in addition to pure number theory, Noether broke new ground in topology during her collaboration with Einstein (Stewart, 2017, pp. 216–19).

Noether's work was so extraordinary that the University of Göttingen welcomed her presence, albeit without faculty appointment. Paid faculty appointment was withheld even though she had the support of the Olympian of mathematicians at the time, David Hilbert, who publicly admitted he was mesmerized by her insights. Hilbert insisted she be treated by fellow mathematicians in every way as a colleague. Yet, even with such support, the university never permitted her to hold faculty rank.

Noether loved mathematics so much, she set aside being the object of bigotry. In fact, she continued to extend the range of her work in mathematics beyond foundations to developing a theorem on symmetry which today remains as one of the most important contributions to theoretical physics ever made (Tent, 2008).

Nothing in the few photographs that remain of her depict the magisterial mind that was never subordinated to another mathematical mind or to another mind in high-energy physics. She herself was a mathematical hero, and every man she worked with, which included most of the leading mathematicians at the time, recognized her as such. Nonetheless, the general prejudice toward women by large university faculties prevented her from ever achieving appropriate faculty rank despite her publication record and acclaim among fellow mathematicians.

Surely such humbling treatment had to be stressful, but not so much that she lost her passion for math, not so much that her personality alignment with the personality of math ever wavered. Oblivious to all but pursuit of mathematical insight, she dressed plainly, wearing giant glasses and presenting a kindly and natural demeanor seemingly unaffected by any ambition other than to understand math and the world governed by math (Posamentier & Spreitzer, 2020).

When the Nazis were desecrating the great universities of Germany (and then Poland, Austria, and elsewhere), Noether was in the most dangerous of all situations. She had no faculty rank, she was a woman, and she was a Jew! She did escape and made her way to America. But, unlike Einstein, Tarski, and so many other internationally famous mathematicians and high-energy physicists, the only position she could obtain in America, even with her publications and degree in hand, was at a small finishing school for women. In 1933 Noether took a position at Bryn Mawr College, but she also lectured at the highly esteemed Institute for Advanced Study in Princeton. Unfortunately, once in America, Noether was absent from the conversations and debates with other champions of math for the last two years of her life. In 1935 she died during cancer surgery.

Noether was in a way abandoned by the mathematical community. There was no effort by the American government to recruit her to any of the many research centers increasingly dominated by the presence of immigrants fleeing the Nazis. She was ignored solely because she was a woman. Neglected as she was, she never forfeited her love and alignment with the mathematical personality. She personified the heroic personality of mathematics in all five features and more.

Her demeanor was similar to that of so many other great minds in mathematics, with the possible exception of flamboyant characters like John von Neumann and Alfred Tarski. Noether was in love with math. She was passionate about finding its secrets. She eulogized nature by demonstrating mathematical accounts of some of nature's most foundational structures. Physicists could discover much of nature's furniture, but it was Emmy Noether who could tell them how that furniture must be arranged.

Looking through the children's collections of hundreds of notable biographies in two large Barnes and Noble stores recently, there was but one book for young readers about Marie Curie, while for older girls there were a couple about Marie Curie, but only one biography of Emmy Noether. Oddly, there were three of Lady Ada!

There are so many more biographies that need to be written about successful women mathematicians and Nobel Laureates. Ada's story is not one of those. Lady Ada's actual history does little to encourage girls to consider a life of mathematical discovery. In this book on the personality of mathematics, there is nothing in Ada's story that is relevant other than to discourage readers from considering her as centrally affiliated with any aspect of the personality of math. In contrast, Emmy Noether was in love with math, while Ada was no more than a groupie of the intellectual elite.

WOMEN AND THIS EMERGING GOLDEN AGE OF MATHEMATICS

Augustus De Morgan, Karl Pearson, Sewall Wright, and Francis Galton were showing how probability could be used to give statistically reliable assessments of much that surrounds human life. Michael Faraday was mathematically organizing the idea of field theory, electromagnetism, and so on, while the logician Charles Dodgson, under the pen name of Lewis Carroll, was writing children's books to entice children into consideration of paradox. Moreover, Giuseppe Peano, Gottlob Frege, Georg Cantor, G. H. Hardy, John Littlewood, Alfred North Whitehead, David Hilbert, Bertrand Russell, and so many others were swirling in a dazzling world of mathematically based achievement.

In this regard, Noether's story is much like the story of Hypatia, the first notable woman mathematician discussed in a previous chapter. Each woman was respected for achievement, but neither was welcomed into the male-dominated world of foundational mathematics. Still, each was so full of passion for the subject that neither could let go.

Why would a supremely talented woman like Noether stay so steadfastly absorbed in mathematics? Surely it could not be because women were treated well in the mathematics community. They might be treated well by those closest to them who admired their prowess, but the international mathematical community often took little notice even when their colleagues tried to share at least some public accolades with them. What kept the few women who persisted? Simply, it was unrelenting passion for the subject.

In the past few years, things have begun to change for women. The first Fields Medal to ever be awarded to a woman was given in 2014 to Maryam Mirzakhani and in 2019 the first Abel prize awarded to a woman was awarded to Karen Uhlenbeck. These prizes are routinely referred to as the "Nobels of mathematics."

Biographies of these women emphasize their passion, not for calculation, but for the search for truth. Each is a hero of the mathematical personality as much as any male hero in mathematical history. The biographies of these women are colorful and available at every reading level from elementary school through high school. (See, for example, *Maryam's Magic: The Story of Woman Mathematician Maryam Mirzakhani* by Megan Reid and Aliya Jaleel, 2021.) The STEM programs using rubric-based processes stressing technology to increase the speed and accuracy of calculation may have razzle-dazzle about them, but they fail to reveal the personality of math and the relevant commonalities in the personalities of heroic mathematicians over the ages.

STEM programs that merely hype some women's success stories in math-driven industries, computing, and business as exhibiting being good at math are reaching low-hanging fruit. Women who became champions of math and STEM interests ought to make their stories available in every math curriculum. Women who unrelentingly refuse to give up serious study have adventurous zeal, courage, and passion for truth, as do all mathematical heroes. Each of these heroines is acting in a way reminiscent of George Mallory's explanation for why he attempted Mount Everest: Because it was there! The challenge of the mathematical wilderness sparks the personality of each man and woman who ever pursued mathematics to Olympian heights.

KEY IDEAS OF CHAPTER 4

1. *Challenge* drives the champions of math, and not merely the view from some intellectual summit.
2. *Making math:* is that something the champions of mathematics do, or is it math itself that turns some people into champions? Becoming a champion of math does not just happen. Not now, not ever.
3. *Making math champions* or even those very good at math begins by inviting them into the Great Conversation of Humankind as the Conversation applies to mathematics. The invitation must begin early and be all- inclusive. There is no magic. Neither man nor woman nor a person of any ethnicity simply becomes privileged in the world of mathematics. And, unlike royalty, no matter how smart one may be, no one simply gets born into mathematics.
4. Hypatia. Emmy Noether. Maryam Mirzakhani. Sofia Kovalevsky. Sophie Germain. Women *champions* weigh in among the best of all mathematicians.
5. *Glass ceilings* hampered women in pursuit of mathematical excellence just as they hampered their progress in the corporate and business worlds. The invitation to mathematical excellence and familiarity with the personality of math must be sustained so that the world is never again at risk of losing the talents of a Noether, a Kovalevsky, or a Johnson.
6. *The mathematical wilderness,* though genuinely infinite in size, is most competently mastered by explorers who fearlessly mount an sustained challenge, venturing into its mysteries with trail-blazing insight.

Chapter 5

Math Problems and the Personality of Math

THE PERSONALITY OF MATH IS REVEALED THROUGH ITS PROBLEMS

There is more to the personality of math than revealed through its champions. The personality of math is also revealed through the problems and achievements marking its history. Great problems of math usually stand outside the world of human sensory experience. People do not see prime numbers, or imaginary, rational, or irrational numbers any more than they *see* natural or so-called counting numbers. Truths about numbers exist and can be grasped by human beings despite the numbers themselves having never been experienced through smells, sights, sounds, taste, or touch.

The language of numbers is more recently evolved than linguistic expression in general. The historical and anthropological records suggests that number talk began as a device for tracking and accounting purposes. The first signs of number talk seem to have been through finger accounting. This may have begun in Babylonia, though some suspect it may have been dated earlier in what is now Turkey (Al-Khalili, 2011). Within a few hundred years number talk and representation appear in India, China, and Mayan cultures (Nieder, 2019).

Here is the first achievement of mathematics. It could be used and symbolized. More astonishing is the fact, nothing short of mind-boggling, that it appeared in several different cultures that never engaged with one another! And, why those cultures and not in others?

Even today there are small cultures that count with finger notation but still have not developed a language of mathematics. The Pirahã for instance, a small tribe in Brazil, do not have a language for math even today, though they do count on their fingers and manage to engage in trade as a result (Nieder, 2019, pp. 83–84).

And the eeriness of all this does not end with the local achievements of vastly separate cultures. When these cultures began engaging one another, math talk seemed as translatable from one culture to another, much as talk about human needs such as eat, sleep, and copulate could easily be translated (Ferreiros, 2016). Can these extraordinary events be explained in evolutionary terms?

The various symbols of math talk varied from culture to culture, but the structural order seemed readily evident in translation. Moreover, as one culture surged a bit ahead in one area of mathematics, this was often found to be quite shareable across cultures, even in antiquity. The Greeks found the practice of proof indispensable to certifying the value of an otherwise intuited theorem such as the Pythagorean theorem. Arab cultures found early algebra to be a ready means for amplifying the potency of mathematics in commerce and astronomy (Berlinski, 1995; Boyer, 1968).

It works, but how do we know it is so?

The formula known today as the Pythagorean theorem was utilized in many cultures as a consequence of personal experience and inventiveness (Maor, 2019). The Greeks thought math seemed so true, it ought to be possible to prove it true. So, proof became an object of mathematical study, not only with regard to the Pythagorean theorem, but also with regard to the status of prime numbers, squaring the circle, infinitesimals, infinities, what we call irrational numbers, and the relation of numbers to geometry. We will turn to each of these topics, sketching first the distraction each posed and how things from antiquity passed into the Middle Ages, the Enlightenment, and beyond.

"PROOFINESS" AND EUCLID'S FIFTH POSTULATE

Islamic algebraists justified their proofs through reference to geometric diagrams. It was not until the late sixteenth century that Enlightenment mathematicians, in Italy especially, began using algebraic symbolism in their proofs. This amplified the potency of algebra and led to the calculus while increasing freedom from the Euclidean geometric model of "proofiness."

Admittedly, Diophantus of Alexandria in the third century CE toyed with the idea of symbolism in his approach to "proofiness," using only +, -, x, ÷. However, this allowed imaginary numbers like the square root of -1 to lurk in the recesses. In about 600 CE, Brahmagupta showed a way to work around the imaginary number in quadratic equations. From Brahmagupta, symbol-based proof travelled to the Islamic world where it was championed by al-Khwarizmi around 800 CE and acquired the name "algebra." Over time these results drifted into the hands of Italian mathematicians during the next seven hundred years.

Despite ingenious work both in algebra and in geometry, for example Descartes's analytic geometry, proof remained rooted in a largely Greek model following Euclid. This was despite continuing concerns about Euclid's fifth axiom, which reads like this as translated in Wikipedia's article on the Parallel Postulate:

> If a line segment intersects two straight lines forming two interior angles on the same side that are less than two right angles, then the two lines, if extended indefinitely, meet on that side on which the angles sum to less than two right angles.

The question was whether this should be treated not as an axiom but rather as itself a theorem (Hales, 2008). But it was not until the late nineteenth century that Beltrami showed that the fifth axiom could be treated nonaxiomatically in non-Euclidian geometries. In addition, in the nineteenh century Dedekind and then Peano discovered a way to shift the focus of proofiness onto arithmetical reasoning by providing a set of axioms for the natural numbers (Peano, 1889).

Part of the momentum toward Dedekind's and Peano's way of thinking is that mathematicians were beginning to envision lines differently than in standard Euclidean plane geometry. The concept of nonparallel lines and geodesics was intriguing to mathematicians and led them to search for new mathematical objects. These objects would turn mathematicians' gaze even more fully toward Plato's bright light behind all previous accomplishments and toward the realm of eternal truths, toward genuine mathematical reality.

PRIME NUMBERS

Prime numbers have delighted and mystified mathematicians since the earliest days of mathematical history (Mazur, 2005). Once again, Euclid beat everyone else to the punch by coming up with a geometric proof of the infinity of prime numbers. More convincing arithmetic proofs followed two millennia later, but all along the infinity of primes was never in doubt, though things sure seemed suspicious. Think about it. Primes are numbers that can only be divided without remainder by 1 and by itself. That alone makes them unique. But there is more. They do not seem to follow any regular pattern.

No one has ever been able to create a formula to predict when the next prime along the number line will show up. Many have tried, but with no success. And matters proved to be yet more complicated. Not only is there no detectable pattern (and you can imagine that fact alone challenges lovers of math), but the distance between primes seems to grow generally larger the further down the number line one goes.

Still there is more. In general, the distance between primes does generally get larger the further one moves along the number line, but there are these occasional pairs of primes separated only by two, like 17 and 19, that show up occasionally. And these rare pairs have been proven to be an infinite set.

And there is even more mystery surrounding the primes. There are primes called Mersenne primes. Marin Mersenne, a seventeenth-century French mathematician and Catholic priest, noticed that primes that were 1 less than any power of 2 had their own special set of additional unique properties (their generic form is $M_n = 2^n - 1$), and an Oxford mathematician, Vicky Neale, recently conjectured that the Mersenne primes comprise another infinite set (Neale, 2017).

The Mersenne primes have yet another characteristic that distinguishes them even among all other primes. They are closely related to what are called "perfect numbers." Perfect numbers are numbers that are equal to the sum of all the positive divisors that you can multiply together to produce them (excluding the number itself). So, 6 is a perfect number because 1, 2, and 3 are divisors of 6, and also $1 + 2 + 3 = 6$. It turns out that 28 is also a perfect number, and it will take just a moment to prove that. Now think more generally. Notice that 6 and 28 are even, and then ask whether there is an odd perfect number. It does not seem to many people that there could be one, but can it be proven one way or another?

And the oddness of these mathematical objects that are primes continues to amaze and inspire lovers of mathematics. Prime numbers are the fundamental building blocks of all numbers. That is right! Any number that is not prime can be made by multiplying prime numbers together. Is this not a world unlike any you, the reader, have ever experienced?

There is a reason why prime numbers have lured devotees into their study for millennia. And, again, this is just one other area of mathematics that students rarely get to see in rubric-driven curriculums that aim at testing for little more than skills of speed and accuracy and application to predictable problem sets.

THE PERSONALITY OF MATH AND SOLUTIONS TO MATH PROBLEMS

The personality of mathematics is revealed here in its foundational problems and commitments, and not in the mere practice of setting up and running equations. In a world governed by so much artificial intelligence, prime numbers have become essential to encryption protection. But such protection rarely if ever leads to a need to primes the size of most Mersenne primes discovered so far. So, why do people keep searching for the next largest Mersenne or more truths about quirky prime properties? They do it because they are intrigued by mystery and challenge and the promise of certainty if they get things right. Herein lies the personality of mathematics, and the math curriculum throughout school needs to open the door to students from time to time to discover this personality.

Surely not everyone needs to become a champion of mathematics, seeking out new insights in every nook and cranny of the mathematical world. But without at least some students pursuing this route, new tools and applications are unlikely to become available to those who competently employ the utility of mathematical discovery to accomplish more in the empirical world that seems so mathematically organized.

Consider this: is it not true that those who understand a discipline's personality are in the best position to be confident in regard to its solutions? For example, in history, those who understand the personality of history know that it must lend itself sooner or later to a narrative.

Moreover, they understand that the narrative relies on evidence, which can make one developing narrative more credible than another. They see history unfolding as the rise and fall of civilizations, novel social or technical initiatives, or, perhaps, as the success of especially talented individuals. Evidence may include carbon-14 dating of archaeological remains, personal letters written at the time, dated news stories, actuarial data, government reports—all things that may underscore moments of an optimally plausible narrative. The tools constructing the best narratives secure the confidence of historians.

In biology, similarly, the power of conceptual tools and empirical observations secure the confidence of biologists. For example, during much of history biologists were tolerant of teleological explanations, explanations in terms of supposed functions or purposes of a feature of an organism, especially in biomedical applications. When new insights into genetics and molecular mechanisms of inheritance became more than just stipulated fact, biologists increasingly gave up teleological explanations and instead sought theories more readily subject to disconfirmation (Segerstrale, 2013).

Even in physics, the most rigorously organized of all sciences, the conceptual tools for organizing and interpreting observations must work to secure the confidence of investigators for further lines of research. The principle of uncertainty, quantum leaps, quanta exhibiting both wave and particle characteristics, new particles only indirectly perceivable, and so on may lead to speculation about gravitrons, string theory, and the like, but always empirical data and rigorously organized inferential protocols are required to secure the conclusions of physicists.

The personality of math (and perhaps theology?) is a bit different. The power of conceptual tools may lead to undeniable conclusions, but ones which nonetheless, at times, leave its champions with the haunting feeling this must make sense but . . . does it really?

Inspired by Euclid, mathematicians have long sought in each area of math for a set of fundamental statements, or axioms, from which all of the truths in that area of math could be deduced. So in the nineteenth century Peano came up with a set of axioms that seemed arguably sufficient to generate all of the truths of arithmetic. But in the twentieth century, Kurt Gödel produced a surprising pair of results. First, he proved that in any formal system system which was consistent, that is, contained no contradictions, and which was sufficient to express the truths of arithmetic, then there are truths expressible in the language of the system that cannot be proven in that system. Second, he proved that such a system cannot prove that it is itself consistent. These are known as Gödel's incompleteness tTheorems, and they have invited much reflection by anyone interested in mathematics and its philosophical underpinnings.

Here is another simpler-seeming puzzle. The set of odd natural numbers and the set of even natural numbers are both the same size: infinite. And, both of those sets are the same size as the set of all natural numbers. Yet the set of all natural numbers seems to swallow each of the other two sets. How can they all be the same size?

The power of the conceptual tools makes their identity of size undeniable. Yet the human mind, bounded in its comprehension, has trouble imagining that one set can swallow another set with no change in size. Infinite sets can be added or subtracted from one another with no change in size, and yet each is a well-defined and distinct set. The personality of math accommodates literally unimaginable truths. Securing confidence in those generatively demonstrable truths can be disturbing, to say the least. This mysterium of math is unmatched by any other traditional school subject discipline. And this mysterium is surely one of the charms leading some to become enchanted and heroic investigators of the mathematical wilderness.

To get a fuller appreciation of how the personality of math has the unusual property of increasing the power and rigor of truth discernment while at the same time it seems to challenge its champions, consider a bit further the puzzles prompted when thinking of infinities.

INFINITIES

If one considers two points on a line, it seems these distances between points could be divided infinitely, and therefore there would never be a true "next to" or "immediately adjacent to" relationship between any two points ever. Conceptually that was very troubling, and there were no tools revealing a solution.

Then consider the triangle created when we start with a square with sides one unit long and we draw a diagonal from corner to corner, cutting the square in half. (For our discussion, we will use modern notation because that makes it much, much easier to write.) Pythagoras's theorem says that the diagonal squared is equal to the sum of the squares of the sides, so, since 1 squared is 1, in this case the diagonal squared = 1 + 1 = 2.

So far so good, but how long is the diagonal itself? It is a number which when multiplied by itself equals two. Now let us try to find it by starting a series of approximations. In modern notation we know for example that 1.41 squared = 1.98 while 1.42 squared = 2.01. So, obviously, the number we are looking for is between 1.41 and 1.42. It turns out that we can continue this process forever without arriving at the *exact* result. And the same issue crops up with other cases, for example, when we start with a square whose sides are two units long.

These inescapable infinities are the occasion for the first serious thought about the possibility of irrational numbers existing. This was not a comforting consideration in the minds of most Greek mathematicians at the time. Sticking to geometry as the source of all justified revelation in math, Euclid showed that he could find the volume of a tetrahedron by reconstructing it into an infinity of prisms. This showed that the concept of infinity could be of practical service in considerations of volume.

Archimedes, too, much to the consternation of his peers, was able to show how to find the area under a parabolic segment by breaking it down to infinitely many triangles. It seemed early on, then, that the useful existence of infinity could not be easily denied.

Talk of infinities has always been at the heart of mathematics, at least since it became recognized as its own discipline and not a mere adjunct to the sciences. So many dead ends have been encountered over the centuries as mathematicians tried again and again to look into the brightest of all lights, the nature of infinity (Wagner, R., 2012).

Of course, things were not that simple. One of the greatest of those hypotheses dealt with the continuum **c**. The continuum, **c**, is the nondenumerable set of all real numbers. This sounds like **c** is the whole kit and kaboodle of the foundational objects in the world of mathematics. Unfortunately, it was not all that. It is a wonderfully powerful mathematical object, but math has many more wonderful objects and she is still just slowly revealing them one by one to her lovers.

Another of math's wonderful and powerful objects are the imaginary numbers (Hersh & John-Steiner, 2011). These are numbers formed by multiplying a real number by the square root of -1, itself represented as *i* (Sandifer, 2007; Stipp, 2017). Together with the real numbers, the imaginary numbers constitute the array of complex numbers. At first, they seemed to be an arbitrary creation, but later they came to play a highly useful role in science and so are taken to be as "real" as the real numbers. Confused yet?

Don't be. This is math seeking names for all of its children (objects). In a human family you have parents, and they may be called Mom and Dad. The children may be called by one name: children. Or it may be convenient to call all the girls together, separating them out from the children which as an entire set may include boys as well. Older children may be designated functionally because of what they can do rather than who they are. So, family names can be used indexically to name objects or groups, or they can be used functionally for ways of completing tasks.

Finite sets have a certain cardinality which is simply the natural number that corresponds on a one-to-one basis with the members of the set. So, when the Boston Celtics are playing a game, the cardinality of the set of players on the court is supposed to be 5. Extending this, Georg Cantor recognized that infinite sets can have the property of cardinality. Thus, the set of all natural numbers has the cardinality represented by Aleph naught, $\aleph_0$. As an aside, note that aleph numbers differ from infinity as employed in algebra and calculus. In algebra and calculus, infinities function as processes and not naming objects (Rashed, 2009).

The even numbers can be put into one-to-one correspondence with the natural numbers, 1 goes with 2, 2 goes with 4, 3 goes with 6, and so on, with the result that the two sets have the same cardinality. What Cantor did that was so striking was to ask whether all of the infinite sets of numbers had the same cardinality. And in a striking achievement, he was able to prove that they do not. This can be put somewhat paradoxically as not all infinities are the same size. Thus the "denumerable" infinities are those that can be put into one-to-one correspondence with the natural numbers, while the "nondenumerable" infinities are those that cannot. Strikingly, the real numbers constitute a nondenumerable infinity. (Heard, 2019). Cantor immediately raised the issue of whether there were sets of some cardinality "in between" the cardinality of the natural numbers and the cardinality of the real numbers. This came to be called "the continuum hypothesis" and vexed Cantor and others.

In 1904, the next International Congress of Mathematics was held in Heidelberg, Germany, and things were about to get a bit rocky. Issues of infinity were not yet settled. And, with Cantor and his wife in the front row, Julius König announced that Cantor's solution to continuum hypothesis was wrong! And, what is more, Cantor's claim that the continuum was an aleph number was wrong as well. While Cantor later proved that the continuum was indeed an aleph number, there remained significant problems with the continuum hypothesis as he had previously admitted (Graham & Kantor, 2009).

Then along came Ernst Zermelo, who claimed he solved the continuum problem using something called the Axiom of Choice. A debate began between Zermelo and three of the most highly revered mathematicians in all of France: Borel, Baire, Lebesgue. All rejected Zermelo's Axiom of Choice suggesting "every choice can be well-ordered" (Zermelo, 1904).

Without going into the details of the Axiom of Choice since this book in not itself a math book but merely a book about the personality of math, suffice it to say, much worry surrounded the idea of choice. Mathematics is supposed to be about the light at the opening of the cave. It is emphatically not about the shadows cast on the wall in front of those chained in Plato's cave, nor is it about *the psychology* of what leads humans to turn their heads about or to focus on the shadows.

The French mathematicians feared Zermelo's Axiom of Choice because in their eyes it threatened to turn mathematicians' focus away from universal truths of mathematics and toward psychology of collective shadow-thinking instead. Zermelo was pressing the question. "What does it mean to choose?" and "Are there any limits to the options choice allows humans in mathematics?" The ontological status of all mathematical objects was at stake!

The mathematician Charles-Emile Picard warned that set theory made mathematics look too much like religion! The French mathematicians furiously fought against the advocates of the Axiom of Choice, such as the German School of Mathematics led by the legendary David Hilbert, and later a French splinter group known collectively as the Bourbaki Group (Graham & Kantor, 2009, pp. 60–62).

The point of all this is to show how *contentious* the intellectual adventures of mathematicians can be. Mathematicians know full well what proof requires. Unlike other scientists who do not prove anything absolutely but only approximate truth or manage a privileged set of beliefs that more closely approximate truth than previous efforts, in math there must be absolute coherence among all that counts as mathematical truth. Contradiction and ambiguities count against legitimate conviction.

Without the conviction of absolute coherence, mathematicians treat all analyses, theorems, conjectures, and so on as hypotheses. Even previous standards of proof can be cast aside when, for example, considerations of curved space force reconsideration of say, Euclid's Fifth Postulate, which was a basis of geometric proof in plane geometry (Mazur, 2005).

This search for universal mathematical truths extending beyond reasonable hypotheses at the time was evidenced when the extraordinary Russian mathematicians took hold of set theory and the theory of transfinite numbers. For them, if an object can be so exactly defined even in the abstract, it became a real object in a Platonic world of ideas. Bugaev, Luzin, Egorov, Nekrasov, and Florensky fought vigorously for this account and even extended it into their religion.

These so-called "Name-Worshippers" were so convinced of the religious and mathematical entanglements of a world of abstract realities that they often had to meet and do their work in secret during the days of the First Russian Revolution in 1905–1906. Nekrasov even found grounds in the Name-Worshipping sect to extend the work of Jacob Bernoulli with regard to the Law of Large Numbers and to discount the utility of the law when applied to human free will. Mathematicians are seeking reliable and timeless truths. They recognize their hypotheses and conjectures may fail along the way, but that is all part of the sport of mathematics.

Matters regarding set theory, transfinite numbers, and other infinity-associated concepts are still far from settled, but progress is being made. The reader here should recognize that embracing the Law of Figuring Things Out *energizes* mathematics. Mathematics embraces its lovers in their hearts and souls. The mathematically minded do not search for mathematical knowledge in the hopes it is a sort of lottery ticket or union card that will one day bring them riches. People fall in love with mathematical adventure in much the same way a naturalist falls in love with the ways of a new forest. In each case the explorers explore simply because they can.

IMAGINARY NUMBERS AND OTHER PROVOCATIVE CONCEPTS

The weakening of confidence in the face of rigorous and revealing argument is not limited to consideration of infinities alone. There are many areas of math equally provocative to the serious intellectual adventurer. Just one quick final example for illustration might help underscore this point. There are many families of numbers: natural, rational, irrational, perfect, prime, and more.

The family of imaginary numbers is formed by multiplying a real number by the square root of -1, represented by i. Mathematicians right up through the nineteenth century attempted to remove imaginary numbers formed with i from math altogether. They attempted to show that any complex number of the form $a + ib$ is equivalent to a statement about real numbers. Getting rid of those complex numbers could be an enormous achievement, simplifying the accumulating clutter surrounding their investigation. Ultimately, however, this effort to dispose of imaginary numbers and their appearance in calculations as complex numbers gave way to the insight that imaginary numbers are not only useful in solving cubic equations, but could lead to calculating solutions to all polynomial equations. This is the fundamental theorem of algebra! Consequently, it seemed undeniable that imaginary and complex numbers have always been part of mathematical reality, whether or not they were recognized as such.

Admittedly, one cannot find i (an imaginary number) on the line of real numbers, since it lies on a line perpendicular to the line of real numbers as its own line of imaginary numbers. Weird? All that this requires of mathematical imagination is that the image of a number line give way to a plane of numbers. Finally, an imaginary number like *the square root of -1* behaves like an ordinary number giving correct results about other ordinary numbers.

With the reality of so-called imaginary numbers in hand, mathematicians were able to advance practical utilization of trigonometry with more potent understanding of the sine and cosine functions, and even create imaginary factorizations

Even as recently as the Enlightenment, Italian algebraists justified the rules of algebra as did their Islamic predecessors by appealing to geometric logic (Stillwell, 2019, p. 21). Geometric knowledge always seemed to back algebraic deductions and modelling. However, as alluded to above, from at least the time of Descartes and beyond, geometry became as dependent on algebra and calculus as so many areas of math had previously depended on testing against the mathematician's imagination of geometric properties.

In the end, the point in this chapter is that, even though the wilderness of math seems to grow exponentially deeper, the champions struggle forward. The personality demands the five features mentioned previously and a keen awareness that in math's deepest sectors, things still might not be as they appear to the first explorers. Moving from being good at math to being very good at math to actually understanding aspects about math that no one but previous champions ever experienced, that challenge is hauntingly mysterious and spectacularly exciting to those able and willing to accept it.

KEY IDEAS OF CHAPTER 5

1. *Personality* is found in every formal discipline. History, physics, biology, all have individuating personalities finding favor in the hearts of some. The same is true of mathematics. However, the search for the personality of math seems particularly obscure to many students in today's world of public education.
2. *Math is a language unto itself.* It names things people may never experience with their senses. But in the world of mathematics these things exist, really and truly exist.
3. *Math is an essential tool.* To the extent that mathematics can be superimposed upon the world of sensuously experienced reality, mathematics

can help set apart, relate, and identify all that exists in a way that, without math, humans could no more understand than does any other species.
4. *Number species are many*. There are perfect numbers, complex numbers, rational numbers, irrational numbers, imaginary numbers, zero, primes, and who knows how many more yet to be found and taxonomized in the mathematical realm.
5. The more one learns about the personality of mathematics, the more its five personality features described in chapter 3 become apparent for those who are its champions.

Chapter 6

Educating for Understanding the Personality of Math

INTRODUCING STUDENTS TO THE ORIGINS OF MATHEMATICAL PERSONALITY

The idea that math has a personality is not new (Osterlind, 2019). The ancient Greeks pondered the almost mystical potency of math to capture the structure and activity of so much around us (Menninger, 1992). Recent scientific studies reveal that number sense is traceable to paths and localization within the brain of many species (Hersh, 1997). The parietal lobe in particular is featured in studies of number sense and in numerical calculation processes both (Beckman, 2020, pp. 118–119).

For example, as Dehaene observes, "we now know that a baby's parietal cortex already corresponds to the number of objects at a location that matches when the adult brain calculates 2 + 2 = 4. This region contains neurons sensitive to the number of objects" (Dehaene, 2020, p. 77).

So, are math-processing brains a wholly novel class of biological calculating mechanism? Does mathematical thinking capacity restructure the architecture of human calculating ability and lead to extraordinary imagining?

LOOK AGAIN TO THE ORIGIN OF MATHEMATICS

Neuroeconomist Paul Glimcher says many animals have a calculating instinct. They calculate expected utility of an undertaking and adjust behaviors moment by moment based on those calculations. For example, the leopard chasing an impala and an outfielder running down a fly ball are both purposeful in calculating behavioral adjustments moment by moment

(Glimcher, 2004; Wagner, 2012), yet neither is running formal equations through their consciousness.

Educational psychologist Barbara Tversky, neuroscientist Stanislas Dehaene, mathematician Keith Devlin, and neuroscientist Andreas Nieder look to evolution and neurophysiology for hints about the nature of mathematical thinking (Dehaene, 2020; Devlin, 2000; Nieder, 2019; Tversky, 2019). And, as with Glimcher, all agree that many species calculate. But, as Francis Su describes, there is much more to thinking in human math than mere calculation (Su, 2020). Among other things, speculation, patience, wonder, and persistence are all essential elements of human math thinking.

Calculations and other mathematical processing require neurological resources of various sorts, and many are shared across species. At the same time, researchers should not anthropomorphize actions of other species as evidence of shared, math-doing physiology. For example, bees construct hexagons in their hives. Flowers exhibit Fibonacci sequences in their petal distribution. In both cases this may be no more than blind evolution free of *math thinking* (Devlin, 2017).

The creation and novel employment of mathematical concepts by humans is well documented (Heaton, 2017). Whether organizing rigorous thinking in science or venturing further into the recesses of math itself, there is evidence that such thinking utilizes both *intentionality* and *artful creation* (Frenkel, 2013).

Primitive peoples long ago and today utilize fingers for calculating even before number systems were written (Richeson, 2019b; Boyer, 1968; Dehaene, 2009). There is, of course, a big gap between the number sense exhibited in finger calculation and say, the theory of transfinite numbers, calculus, Bayesian statistics, and more. The fact that some peoples never moved beyond finger math indicates progress in mathematical thinking is neither determinate nor inevitable. Some unusual and special things must happen to catapult mathematical understanding forward (Dehaene, 1997).

In late 2020 the foundation of the largest Mayan structure ever was discovered. There are the Egyptian pyramids, the sacrificial temples in Turkey, and numerical counts of hunts appear in cave dwellings throughout Europe, India, and China, nearly everywhere larger cultures came into being (Courant & Robbins, 1996). As educational psychologist Barbara Tversky and others (Tversky, 2019) point out, numerical figuring beyond mere calculation of cost/benefit is ubiquitous, both historically and still in primitive societies today (Davis & Hersh, 1981).

Much is made of the influence of language in evolutionary history. In addition to linguistic expression, the language of math too evolves and plays a determining role shaping cultures around the world (Wiley, 2015). For example, the Roman Empire stalled in its mathematical investigations because of its awkward mathematical representations. In contrast, Arabic and Indian cultures continued their ascendancy, perhaps because of having a more useful system of representation (Du Sautoy, 2021).

Yet despite cultural variances in number systems employed, philosopher of science Ian Hacking observes, "Deep in human nature is the sense of symmetry . . . intensely investigated by cognitive psychologists" (Hacking, 1990, pp. 171–72). In other words, the structure of math may be endemic to human thinking, but local progress within cultures may advance variably due to things such as conveniences of number representation.

As an example, the theorem attributed to Pythagoras is still taught in classrooms around the world. It is useful in activities from creating the magisterial architecture of great buildings to the more humble tasks of laying carpet or shingling a roof. Pythagoras was fascinated that a mathematical structure seemed to underlie all creation, from the harmonic sounds of lyre strings to the proportionate heights of buildings, mountains, shadows, and so much more. He was a rock star in his day and developed a cult of followers. Followers believed he was illuminating the world before them as no one before ever had. And, importantly, the language of illumination lay in what he was able to do with it in mathematical thinking about the world.

The potency of mathematical constructions reveals aspects of the world otherwise unaccounted for, and this has led to a mysticism surrounding the nature of math ever since. Those such as Pythagoras and his followers who were on the inside creating math may have felt they were masters of a new "mindscape" inaccessible to the untutored. Imagine their excitement!

A NOTE ON THE CONTOURS OF THE MATHEMATICAL WILDERNESS

Moving into the modern era, there has been an explosion of number families and functional processing (Aczel, 2011). From the counting numbers and debates over zero and negative numbers, adventures into the mathematical wilderness evolved, ferreting out insights into rational numbers, irrational numbers, real numbers, imaginary numbers that are the square roots of negative numbers like i (which is the square root of -1), complex numbers, transcendental numbers such as π and e, factorials expressed with $!$ typed next to a natural number, and more. People "good at math" will recognize some of these, and work with some. Those "very good at math" may do well with all or most of these numeric thickets.

And there is yet more to this wilderness; for example, functions cut through it all. Functions include such things as arithmetic's adding, subtracting, multiplying, and dividing, which even those who never went beyond the earliest indoctrination in math learned in elementary school. And then there are functions such as sine and cosine functions, functions resembling computational algorithms, and many, many more. We are not going to go into depth on any of these. For this discussion of the personality of math, it is only necessary that the reader appreciates the depth of the wildernesses to be explored and reasonably anticipates that there is so much more adventurers may one day bring to light.

Those "good at math" have crossed thresholds into one or two of the above number realms and functions. Those "very good at math" have crossed several thresholds both within the realms and often across several. The heroes of math have passed threshold after threshold, finding ever more about math to intrigue them further.

INTRODUCING STUDENTS TO TYPES OF MATHEMATICAL CHAMPIONS

In addition to thinking about mathematics and its uniqueness to humans generally, consider the sorts of problems that seem so alluring to those who become mathematical champions (Zellini, 2020). For convenience, mathematical champions are taxonomized here into three groups. As indicated above, while all mathematicians share much in judgment and aesthetic taste, there is more to the accommodating personality of a math champion.

To start, "champions of mathematics" refers herein to those accomplished figures setting them apart from the crowd of those merely mathematically competent. These champions are further distinguished as: purist, applied, and epistemic champions.

The purists. Purists are ablaze with the passion of discovery into the transcendent mysteries and structure of mathematics unrelated to any obvious application in the physical world.

The applied champions are those who sense in mathematics a key to unlocking the arrangements and processes the material world (Ellenberg, 2021; Yau & Nadis, 2019). Any phenomenon without a mathematical explanation prompts them to begin imagining novel formulas for illuminating hitherto unseen architectures in the surrounding world.

Finally, there are epistemic mathematicians. These champions focus on excellence in making inferences to increase the human knowledge base more generally, and their investigations are largely inductive in nature. Whereas purists focus on understanding the sublimities of math itself, epistemic champions employ math to increase success in creating probabilistic descriptions of the world.

Taxonomies must be treated with a certain amount of tentativeness. Taxonomies are human artifacts. As a consequence, they risk summative error due to ambiguity, vagueness, interpretive equivocation, and such. So it is with this proposed threefold taxonomy. Some champions, for example, do not fit well into just one of the three categories of champions above but rather transcend them in both success and ambition. In addition, some champions may start as purists who stay in love with mathematics, but find themselves drawn by happenstance into sectors of investigation they had not previously contemplated. Several such champions will also be noted below as heuristically revealing.

A historically famous example of a purist mathematicians is Plato (Mazur, 2005). Plato was convinced that there were forms of thought that at best could only be approximately instanced in the world in which humans live. For example, forms such as geometric figures exist perfectly in the world of the abstract, but never in the world of human experience.

Equally paradigmatic is Georg Cantor, who used set theory to illuminate constructions exhibiting truths of infinity. Think too of Kurt Gödel, who proved that any consistent system of mathematics must be incomplete in that the truths of the system cannot be deduced from the principles of the system alone (Goldstein, 2005; Nagel & Newman, 2002; Wang, 1996). This purists' world is beyond the world detectable by human senses. Yet to some, the world of mathematics beyond the world of sensuous detection is all the more real because of that inaccessibility to corrupting distractions of material world experience.

A feature of purists is that they sort through properties of numbers, functions that do not appear to be invented and seem indispensable to math nonetheless. For example, from human number sense came calculations as early as 40,000 BCE (Wagner, R., 2017). Notches on sticks, arrangements of stones, and finger and toe counting indicated that calculations of quantity were evidently commonplace around the world. And, to the purist, tools of calculation create possibilities that flag a world of number-meaning, a world beyond the immediately detectable sensations of material experience.

When it became apparent that culturally determined methods of calculation were reducible to one another, recognition that there are properties of numbers and families of numbers began to appear. The fact that number families and their properties were noted unevenly across cultures did not prevent astute thinkers from recognizing that across cultures, the ostensible meaning of those properties was preserved, even when only vaguely identified in the originating culture.

Beginning with the natural or counting numbers, genuine mathematical insights became readily shared across cultures. Yet inevitably, in a short time appreciation for the apparent weirdness of number secrets began to appear.

For example, the weirdness of positive and negative numbers appeared troubling. Numbers such as 1, 2, 3, . . . , n seem transparent and aligned with the world as it is. But it seemed odd to count -1, -2, -3, . . . and so on. Moreover, bringing positive and negative numbers together into a common theory of number-meaning seemed almost perverse.

Subtraction made sense. A person has nine sheep and sells one. If he subtracts one from his herd, that leaves eight. But saying that the selling of one sheep is equivalent to adding -1 to the herd of 9 seemed pointless and convoluted at first. In addition, the very idea of negative numbers, provoked other problems for separating, matching, or working with both negative and positive numbers together. When a positive quantity, say 2, was combined with a negative quantity, say -2, what was left? Nothing? Does nothing matter? As it turns out, in math nothing *does* matter. It matters enough to have a mathematical name. This led to the challenge of making sense of a concept of nothingness that matters. This challenge led to five hundred years of debate from Greece to China, to settle the problem of a number now named "zero."

Ordinary people may think there should be no problem with zero. To them, zero just means nothing—end of story. But to mathematicians, if zero is a number, then shouldn't it behave as do all the other counting numbers (Hersh & John-Steiner, 2011)? And, if it does not behave like all other counting numbers, does it make sense to describe it as a number at all?

Add 2 + 2 and you get 4. Add 2 + 0 and you get 2. Is that not where you started? So, zero doesn't really matter right? And, when you subtract zero from 2, you are again back where you started. And so again, zero seems not to matter. "So, what is the problem?" (Aczel, 2015). If you add and subtract nothing, why would you expect anything to change? And if nothing changes, what is there to matter?

Multiply 2 by 0 (2 x 0) and something happens; you get less than 2. You now have, nothing . . . whatever that might mean. What happened to the value of 2? When you take the square of 4 (4 x 4), you get 16n. Square 0 (0 x 0) and what do you get? Nothing. The outcome is nothing bigger and nothing smaller. When you divide 0 by any other number you get 0, but any number divided by 0—what does that even mean? The great mathematician Leonhard Euler thought that the answer was infinity (Martinez, 2011).

The fact of the matter is that mathematicians identified further flawed consequences if Euler's conclusion about dividing by 0 was allowed. So now the common wisdom is that dividing by 0 is "undefined." In mathematics, the notable stature of an authority doesn't make a claim right or even advisable to follow. In math, *arguments* are required to secure functions, formulas, equations, and proofs (Martinez, 2012, p. 83). So, does zero matter or not? It matters a whole lot. It matters that we get it right because it has reverberation for all other numbers. We have talked about the infinitesimals between any two counting numbers, for example. But what happens to infinitesimals in the direction from a value of 1 to 0? If the infinitesimals are approaching nothing (0), then why can't the infinitesimals run out and reach nothingness?

The more you think about zero, the less it looks like all the other natural counting numbers. To say it counts for nothing seems like a trivialization to some and perhaps as an oxymoron to math specialists. And the confusion does not end there. At around the same time that folks were trying to figure out what to do about zero (Seife, 2000; Kline, 1972), they had to struggle as well with the idea of negative numbers. People today are so indoctrinated to the notion of negative numbers that they tend to think it is just counting backwards from zero, but is that all there is?

If zero is not a number, then how can you count back from it? Indeed, what is the number to the left of a positive 1 (+1) on the number line? If there is no zero, then it must be negative 1, that is, if negative numbers exist. Say negative numbers exist. If negative numbers exist but zero does not, what happens? $-1 + 1 = ?$ Maybe we should say zero exists and just bring all this confusion to an end. But, given the Law of Figuring Things Out, which supervenes upon all productive thinking, the decision of what to do cannot just be based on convenience (Wagner & Fair, 2020). We are not at liberty to just invent an answer. Mathematicians must figure out what is true about zero, negative numbers, positive numbers, and the properties of each.

The conclusion reached after five hundred years of debate is that zero is something. It is something far more profound than the colloquial term "nothing" can account for. And as it turns out, when 0 is understood as a number, not only does it lead the way for the discovery of quadratic equations, but it also allows for interesting insights into geometric figures.

Then all is good, right? The champions of math have completed their work and all the rest is left is for those "very good at math" to calculate the details, right?

No.

Even the ancient Greeks aware of paradoxes mentioned earlier in this book recognized that there had to be fractional numbers between each pair of counting numbers. But, how many between each pair? How small can the fractions get when they disappear into some absolute number?

The problem was that there appeared no smallest infinitesimal. They appeared to go on forever in an infinity of ever smaller fractions parsed between any two adjacent natural whole numbers. When will all this stop?

Even the Greeks of antiquity who took to going beyond mere arithmetic and geometry and ventured into early analysis ran from the challenge of infinitesimals (Boyer, 1968). Solving the challenge of infinitesimals was too much to ask—at the time. The problem of infinitesimals never went away. It lingered. The Law of Figuring Things Out, however, demands that in math such problems cannot be ignored indefinitely. There must be a way of figuring out what is going on in the fractional world and how this might affect all the rest of mathematics. These challenges affected purists in mathematics, but they also disturbed champions of mathematics, such as those in the next group designated as applied mathematicians.

Paradigmatic of applied champions of mathematics are figures such as Isaac Newton and Claude Shannon. Isaac Newton as co-developer of the calculus (along with Leibniz) was an ethereal thinker writing more on theology than on any other subject. Nonetheless, his work on the calculus had the practical effect of making more understandable the astronomical observations of Copernicus and Kepler. Similarly, Claude Shannon sorted out how information could be detected amid the noise of electronic transmission of data (Nahin, 2012). Shannon used math to clean noise out of the processing of data using programmed redundancy and other techniques. Both men are champions of mathematical excellence, and both used their excellence to unlock mysteries of real-world phenomenon.

One champion who crossed lines in this taxonomy is Emmy Noether. Noether's excellence in pure math helped physicists better organize data they were recovering experimentally but did not know how to aggregate effectively. Another is Leonhard Euler, who is credited, for example, with creating graph theory in pure mathematics, while making contributions to applied areas in physics, astronomy, and music theory, among other applications.

Of course, Carl Gauss, characterized by mathematical historian E. T. Bell as the "prince of mathematics" (Bell, 1957), advanced number theory in pure mathematics and contributed directly to a number of applied sciences. For example, the Gaussian distribution, or so-called "normal" curve in statistics, is today a basic conceptual tool of biomedical science.

THE PURISTS

There are many purists who could be included, so we will only mention a few. The reader should be aware that there is an abundance of literature on mathematical purists such as Andrew Weil, Maryam Mirzakhani, Srinivasa Ramanujan, Shing-Tung Yau, G. H. Hardy, Lord Bertrand Russel, Alfred North Whitehead, Maria Gaetana Agnesi, David Hilbert, Alonzo Church, Madhava of Sangamagrama, Paul Erdös, and many others.

Plato, the paradigmatic purist, thought math and, in particular, the study of geometry gave insight into the truly real. Indeed, unverifiable legend has held for centuries that over the doorway to the Academy was an inscription which, when translated, is "Let no one ignorant of geometry enter." For Plato, human senses can mislead. Real truth exists beyond the senses. No one can draw a perfect circle; we can only approximate one. In Plato's *Meno*, a slave boy with the aid of a few prompts grasps an insight into a general truth about certain geometric figures. For Plato and his descendants, such abstraction alone is the source of genuine truth.

Purists are fascinated by a world of abstraction. In the world of appearances, geometric figures are readily apparent. Yet no humanly experienced circle has exactly 360 degrees. Only abstract, perfect circles placidly imposed in Euclidean planes have 360 degrees. Similarly, angles of a triangle add up to 180 degrees again only in perfect abstraction of Euclid's plane geometry.

In the world of curved space that Lobachevsky, Bolyai, Gauss, and Riemann variously describe, there are no triangles of 180 degrees! In their curved space geometries, convex and concave curved space is ubiquitous. Even at the smallest distance between two material points, however small, the distance is curved. Every such line is a geodesic, thus making all triangles greater than or less than 180 degrees—never the 180 degrees as in the space described by Euclid (Posamentier & Spreitzer, 2020, pp. 19–25). Consider a further example. $A = \pi r^2$ is not a fact of the area of any *experienced* circle. The equation is about the ideal of circle-ness, not *about* real-world appearances. Even the number π identifies no quantity ever experienced directly. Rather it is a property of perfect geometric abstraction.

Maria Gaetana Agnesi is the first woman to have authored a textbook on mathematics and to do so in her own name. Agnesi is often cited as a prototypical feminist. Surely many readers of this book identify with such inclinations. But there is more to Agnesi. She was driven to investigate math and science in order to find her way closer to God (Mazzotti, 2015). In this her motivation echoes Plato.

Plato's thinking of other-worldly and majestic perfection in mathematical abstraction continues to the present day in the work of Kurt Gödel, the greatest logician of the last century, and in the work of Fields medalist nominee Grigori Perelman today (Yau & Nadis, 2019, pp. 240–42). The point is that all pure mathematics, including even probability theory, is separate and apart from the application of mathematical tools used to study real-world phenomena (Berlinski, 1995).

In the famed Moscow School of Mathematics that developed at Moscow University in the early twentieth century, purists such as Nicolai Luzin, Dmitri Egorov, and Father Pavel Florensky did extraordinary work in abstract mathematics while also contemplating the abstract effect of bringing entities into existence by naming and defining alone. This practice was common in their constructivist mathematical approach and their deeply Russian Orthodox religious leanings (Graham & Kantor, 2009).

One of the most famous purists in all history was Sofia Kovalevskaya, whom we discussed in chapter 4. Another purist of extraordinary skill and fortitude was Emmy Noether, whom we also discussed in chapter 4. Then there is the phenomenal Srinivasa Ramanujan. Ramanujan may be India's greatest mathematician ever. This is high praise, since India has produced so many extraordinary mathematicians.

Ramanujan's purist disposition is captured in his practice of seemingly divining interesting formulas and functions without much mathematical training. He lacked familiarity with conventional symbols, and he had little appreciation for proof. Ramanujan claimed his ideas simply came to him as his mind rested on the horizons of the mathematical wilderness. For example, in 1904 he conjured what has come to be known as the Ramanujan constant. This constant is the unique positive zero of the logarithmic integral function. Several years later when he wrote to Britain's great purist, G. H. Hardy, he included the constant as one of his formulaic findings.

The reader need not know the details of the constant for this book, but do know that it can only be approximated to 14 digits by his formula (Hand, 2014, p. 173)! It is a really big number, and he figured out how to generate it while a seemingly inconsequential student in a particularly impoverished area of India.

Hardy arranged for Ramanujan to come to Cambridge University to work with him in pure mathematics. How did Ramanujan come up with such dramatic and powerful insights? Like Emmy Noether, Ramanujan was on fire with a passion for the unexplored wilderness of mathematical structure. They both burned with a sense of zeal and adventure when exploring this abstract wilderness.

In the middle of the twentieth century, Kurt Gödel was similarly affected with an unrelenting zeal and a disciplined sense of adventure for exploring the wilderness of abstract mathematical structure. He most famously came to be known for his "incompleteness" proof which demonstrated that no system of arithmetic can ever be demonstrated to be both complete and consistent. This breathtaking demonstration continues to tantalize mathematicians, philosophers, and computer scientists. It is interesting that this obsession with the abstract led Gödel to contemplate a proof for God toward the end of his life.

The last purist we will note is a contemporary. His name is Grigori Perelman. Perelman lives in New York City. He occasionally teaches, but not often. Remember David Hilbert mentioned earlier? Hilbert had presented at the 1900 International Congress of Mathematicians in Paris ten of a longer list of mathematical problems. These challenging problems generated a large amount of creative mathematical work. In 2000 the Clay Mathematics Institute followed Hilbert's example by proposing a set of seven Millennium Prize problems, and set up million-dollar prizes for anyone who could solve one of the problems. Perelman solved two, but he refused the money. Perelman was also named a Fields medalist. This is akin to the Nobel prize for mathematics, but again, Perelman refused to accept the honor. Why?

His explanation for refusing was that, unlike an engineer or scientist, he never invented anything. All he did was to discover what had been there all along and so he was undeserving of any awards or rewards. Perelman regards the world of abstract mathematics as very real. He is passionate about finding his way about in that world.

These brief notes on the purists show that beyond extraordinary intelligence, these champions of mathematics exhibit an adventurer's zeal for exploring an untouched wilderness. They revel in the challenge of finding their way about this abstract wilderness. Each is different from the other in many ways but zeal, adventuring into the unknown, and the courage to stay with it reflect central features of these mathematicians and too, the allure of the discipline itself. People often talk about the beauty of mathematics. But the allure is not sufficiently potent to account for the fierce zeal and dedication of the champions.

Mathematicians can be roughly divided up between those who are focused on pure mathematics and those who focus on application. Such distinction is admittedly rough. For example, even in the case of the high-minded G. H. Hardy, who criticized his protégé Norbert Wiener for doing applied mathematics, Hardy himself was lured into applied math by a biologist needing help to create a formula useful in sorting through issues of population genetics. The resulting formula is the still famous Hardy-Weinberg equation (Hardy, 1967).

Other mathematicians are preoccupied with bringing mathematics into their effort to unlock the keys of understanding the universe. Are these applied mathematicians so different from the purists such that the discipline's personality is seen differently by them? Let us take a look.

THE APPLIED CHAMPIONS

Mathematics makes possible the organization of thinking by those who want to understand the world more generally. Without mathematics it would be all but impossible to aggregate large amounts of data and interpret suggestive patterns revealing how the world works, often in ways other than the most obvious appearances.

The Greeks were not the only ones to discover that mathematical applications opened up doors in the here and now. For example, in the Arab world, Muhammad ibn Musa al-Khwarizimi wrote *On Calculations* with Hindu numerals, and in the treatise, he laid out the first recorded version of working with algorithms and began the first explorations into algebra. His algebra showed what can be learned by adding the same term to both sides of an equation. His work was as significant as that of the Chinese mathematicians at a time when Europe was handicapped by the use of Roman numerals (Rashed, 2009).

Liu Hui in the third century BCE wrote the first masterpiece in Chinese mathematics. In it he produces something that looks like the Pythagorean theorem, yet it was developed wholly independent of Greek influence (Stewart, 2017, pp. 21–27). Another Chinese mathematician of roughly the same period, Chang Heng, explored the extraction of roots and the solution of simultaneous equations. Chou Chun, another mathematician of the time, constructed a method for solving quadratic equations. Other Chinese mathematician included Liu Hsin and Tsu Ch'ung Chih, who lived at different times but both calculated useful values for π. Greeks and Chinese thousands of miles apart and with no cultural interchange were finding their way to what increasing look like universal truths accessible only by rigorous thinking.

By the Middle Ages the great work by Indian mathematicians was becoming well known, first through Brahmagupta, then Parameshvara Nambudiri, Madhava of Sangamagrama, and Nilakantha Somayaji, and perhaps most importantly, Melpathur Narayana Bhattathiri, the author of what some call—rather than Leibniz and Newton—the first calculus text. And on the other side of the globe throughout all this time there were sophisticated astronomical calculations being produced by Aztec and Mayan scholars, but no reliable record of who wrote what exists (Berlinski, 1995).

Consider the development of algebra. Muhammad al-Khwarizmi was probably the first to imagine a mathematical construct for organizing logistics in trade. In fact, when Europeans learned algebra from the Middle East, they took to calling it algebra after this originating champion's book that had *al-jabr* meaning "completion" or "rejoining" in its title. More than a millennium later, the attorney and amateur mathematician, George Boole, set out to use algebra to organize what he thought were the "laws of thought"—or at least the laws of systematic thought. Boolean algebra became the foundation of much computer programming a century after Boole died. Boolean algebra remains central to much work in computer programming today.

More recently, beginning in the 1940s under the tutelage of John von Neumann and Oskar Morgenstern, mathematical game theory, a new way of formalizing the laws of best practices for thinking in social interactions, was initiated (Helms, 1980). And with the advent of powerful computers, game theory is currently exploited by financiers, economists, mathematical biologists, poker devotees, chess masters, and many others to exhibit the most potent strategies for negotiation, war, and evolutionary survival.

The idea of using math to unlock nature had been around for a long time. But as humans got better at math and in making systematic observations of nature, nature seemed to grow more stubborn in giving up her secrets. Galileo's utilization of detailed records and mathematical treatment of data when considering such things as the behavior of a pendulum were impressive enough, but eventually scientists, looking at more detail in nature, concluded that it required consideration of odd things such as infinitesimals and continuous modeling of surfaces, lines, and other patterns.

Isaac Newton and Gottfried Leibniz independently invented the calculus, "flattening the curve" as it was then called. The calculus rendered ever more trustworthy interpretations of continuous data configurations. Previous attempts to flatten the curve always relied on moving toward infinitesimally smaller line segments that when added together gave a range of the numerical value of area contained within or below the curve. Certainty was still elusive but the approximations achieved were beyond anything previously imagined. The calculus escaped the distraction of infinitesimals for the time being. The calculus made possible figuring out the path of a continuous function, revealing more likely profiles of data aggregation without securing absolute certainty (Berlinski, 1995; Stewart, 2017).

Newton was not caught up in pure mathematics for its own sake. He was obsessed with reality, which for him meant the world of experience and the presence of its creator. Two-thirds of all his writing was theology, not science or math (Iliffe, 2017). His calculus, like his laws of motion and gravity, reflected a desire to use math to open doors to what he took to be the created world. In a sense for Newton, God was a mathematician, and the key to understanding God better was to use the creator's language, math, to unfold the layout of the universe.

Two other applied mathematicians working at the same time were Blaise Pascal and Pierre Fermat. These two scientists are the founders of decision-making under conditions of uncertainty (Devlin, 2008; Hacking, 1990). Through his correspondence with Pierre Fermat, Pascal *figured out* that tools taken from probability theory could be employed to increase the effectiveness of making decisions under conditions of uncertainty such as those at the gambling table (Spiegelhalter, 2020, p. 213; Stewart, 2017, pp. 53–56).

These applied mathematicians showed how probabilistic formulas could better manage risk-taking, from how best to ensure cargo transport to stabilizing logistical support of armies (Posamentier & Spreitzer, 2020, pp. 75–84). Other applied mathematicians such as Pierre-Simon Laplace and the Bernoulli family appropriated tools of mathematical probability to make plausible decisions in the turbulent world of commerce, astronomy, meteorology, artillery accuracy, and even applied public health (Posamentier &

Spreitzer, 2020). These are practical affairs, not explorations of the abstract itself. Uncertainty haunts applied math—unlike proofs in formal math.

About applying abstract formalizations to real-world scenarios, Hans Halverson aptly warns, "At best, logic [math] can help us to calculate the costs of our beliefs . . . it is up to you to decide what costs you are willing to pay" (Halverson, 2020, p. 225).

Albert Einstein was a superb applied mathematician. He solicited the help of geometer Bernhard Riemann to construct the non-Euclidean world of special relativity theory, but it was the world itself he wanted to understand and not the abstractions of mathematics by themselves. This is characteristic of all champions of applied mathematics. Applied mathematicians may wax eloquently about the beauty of mathematics, but their praise is really for the potency of math to reveal the underlying beauty of the world (Devlin, 2000).

At present we have a world of algorithms, calculations, and artificial intelligence all aimed at forcing nature to submit to the control of human imagination. This world is a world of information. Indeed, mathematical physicist David Deutsch has gone so far as to speculate that information is the most fundamental piece of nature's anatomy (Deutsch, 2011).

No one has done more to highlight information as central to unlocking hidden insights into the world than Claude Shannon. Claude Shannon is known as the father of information theory. Information for Shannon, and all scientists since, is the rule-governed manipulation of symbols. Sounds like math, right? That is because information theory is math.

Shannon set out originally to figure out a metatheory for governing the regulatory pathways of electricity currents in order to diminish the amount of noise in telephone communications. Now all electrical transmissions and communication models reflect Shannon's construction of information theory as the most productive insight into nature's transmissions and rendering of substance into worldly realization. Shannon's genius was of mythic proportions for much of the twentieth century, and that continues to this very day (Shannon & Weaver, 1949). To understand Shannon's embrace of the mathematical personality, it is perhaps best to describe his later collaboration with another champion of mathematics, Edward Thorp.

Edward Thorp is perhaps most famous for his card-counting strategy and method for breaking the bank at several casinos, all certainly based on the application of math to real-world phenomena (Thorp, 2017). But Thorp is so much more than a mathematical game theorist. He started a Ph.D. in physics, but learned it would take too long to get the degree and cost money he did not have. So, he switched to mathematics.

Thorp used his mathematics degree for fun and profit, but always in an applied sense. He became a professor of mathematics and published substantial work. But behind it all was always the desire to lift up nature's curtain and see the Big Show for real. Besides beating Las Vegas casinos in blackjack, he made a fortune on the stock market, ultimately creating his own unparalleled success as a hedge fund manager. Thorp has lived well due to his applied mathematical genius, but, like so many mathematical superstars, money was not as appealing as mathematical adventure (Thorp, 2017). He gave much of his money to universities.

Mathematical adventure is what brought Thorp together with Claude Shannon. Thorp always admired Shannon and loved the quirky stories one would hear about Shannon riding a unicycle down the halls of Bell Labs while juggling balls and thinking about applying math to this or that mystery. Thorp had an idea that he thought would be fun—so much fun that he might be able to entice the fabled Shannon to join him on a quest to use math to expose yet more of what others presumed was just chance.

Thorp went to MIT where Shannon was a professor at the time, and he proposed they work together to figure out how to outmaneuver roulette wheels in Las Vegas. Thorp was timid about proposing the idea to the grand master, but Shannon loved it! As applied mathematicians, neither thought in terms of perfect die or other abstractions of some Platonic heaven. Roulette wheels were human artifacts subject to imperfection. Figure out the imperfections of any one roulette wheel, and a person should be able to calculate how to do better than chance in winning at that wheel.

Shannon was so enthralled with the idea he bought the finest-made roulette wheel he could find and had it installed in his basement. He and Thorp spend hours spinning the wheel and tabulating the results. They came up with a formula that proved effective, albeit modestly so. Still, the adventure and the success were sufficient for the zeal that motivated each to continue looking to unlock more of nature's secrets using mathematics rather than creating new math.

What do we learn about the personality of math from these champions of applied math? Applied mathematicians are adventurers! And they use the abstract to capture penetrating insights into all that is real. Remember Pascal and his use of probability tools to make better judgements under conditions of uncertainty?

Pascal was so smitten with the potency of math that he constructed a probabilistic account of why one should believe in and live to satisfy a creator God. As already admitted, champions of applied math must always live with some degree of uncertainty in their applications. So, Pascal's and even Newton's ventures into the supernatural were not seeking mystical experiences, but they were instead efforts to penetrate further into what they considered reality. Their confidence that reality could be laid open for investigation through math is testimony to their continued zeal and unrelenting spirit of wanting to figure things out. It is also testimony to their commitment, implicit or otherwise, that all that existed was in fact organized mathematically (Suppes, 1984, 2001).

THE EPISTEMIC CHAMPIONS

The epistemic champions of mathematics are first and foremost epistemologists, those whose goal is to develop an understanding of what knowledge is and how best to acquire it. First and foremost, they are concerned with making exacting inferences that best approximate how the world is laid out and with identifying trends of how it might be evolving. In short, they see in mathematics a resource for making more robust *inductive* inferences.

The most exacting procedures for making inductive inferences come from the field of statistics. Lay people often confuse statistics and probability. Statistics is about figuring out the world by analyzing and understanding patterns in data, while probability is about abstract mathematical arrangements of ideal configurations. Much like developing our understanding of geometry by starting with Euclid's axioms, our understanding of probability can be developed by understanding the implications of a set of axioms such as those put forth by Komolgorov in 1933.

As noted above, Pascal, Fermat, the Bernoullis, and others were among the first to see that mathematical tools of probability could illuminate realms of previously impenetrable uncertainty. Statistician David Spiegelhalter aptly notes that majority of the mathematical tools used in statistics were produced in the fifty years after Pascal and Fermat (Spiegelhalter, 2020, p. 207).

Inasmuch as induction was famously pursued as an object of study by philosophers and economists such as David Hume, John Stuart Mill, John Maynard Keynes, Frank Ramsey, and others, it is tempting to separate theorists of induction from statistical theorists. This is an unnecessary and misleading taxonomic bifurcation, as will soon become clear.

In the physical sciences, Galileo opened the door to sampling summaries in statistical reasoning. But it was Ludwig Boltzman's study of gases that led to physics widely adopting statistical management of data. By Boltzmann's time, the purist mathematician Carl Gauss had already noticed that distribution of many common characteristics lend themselves to representation in what looks like a bell-shaped curve. This normal curve and the associated concept of standard deviation from the mean gave descriptive statistics a credible boost as a set of tools for thinking along the line of truth-approximating knowledge.

Gauss, along with Adrien-Marie Legendre, added the concept of *line of best fit* marking out an aggregation of data along an X/Y axis. If the data points look something like a pointillist painting of a football by Georges Seurat, the line of best fit runs neatly through the middle of the football, bifurcating the plotted data points. If the arrangement of data points looks chaotic, then there may be no line of best fit and no positive evaluations to be construed (Spiegelhalter, 2020, p. 125).

During this same time, Charles Darwin's cousin, Francis Galton, measured everything he could imagine. He even began considering comparative measurements of intelligence (Gould, 1981). Galton's work illustrates how formulas can be potent assets when aggregating and comparing data, even when the data dictate no certain insights into the world.

Consider Galton's discovery of *regression to the mean* (Galton, 1877). Men are typically taller than women, and there are geographic differences between groups of men and women in mean difference in height. Tall parents usually have tall children, but rarely are the children as tall as the parents themselves, and thus the children are closer to, that is, regressing to, the mean. Short parents tend to have short children, but not as short as they themselves.

It seemed to Galton as if nature was in the business of righting some imbalances. Galton's formula for regression to the mean was not intended to be a work of mathematics, but rather an invention to track observations more systematically (Galton, 1877, pp. 492–95). Galton then figured out that regression was apparently common throughout much of observed reality. This is a paradigmatic episode of how statistics *utilized* math to fulfill robust epistemic ambitions (Stigler, 1989, pp. 73–86).

Galton also considered other statistical measurements, such as the median. Medians slice through data, setting the *number* of observations from smallest to largest equally on either side of the midpoint, which is the median. Then there is the mode. The mode is the numerical quantity that most frequently appears in a set of data. The mode and median add useful ways for characterizing sampled populations in addition to the mean, but they are not themselves *mathematical* advances.

Following a short time after Galton, Karl Pearson and his son Egon Pearson made a case for something called *the correlation coefficient r*. This is still today referred to as the Pearson correlation coefficient. The correlation coefficient modelled associations that, while not causal, seemed more intimately associated then mere coincidence.

The correlation coefficient added to the statistical toolbox another metric improving epistemic judgement about the relationship between two groups (Pearson, 1900, pp. 157–75). But correlation coefficients can only take researchers so far (Neyman & Pearson, 1933, pp. 289–37). Correlations raise fruitful suspicions, but for suspicions to become more epistemically accountable they must possess degrees of validity and reliability as part and parcel of systematic, real-world observations.

Edging closer to the twentieth century, statistical applications in public health made entire new sciences possible: epidemiology, meteorology, and population genetics. There are many examples showing how statistical applications improved public health. Consider the following three from epidemiology.

In Soho, an area of London, an outbreak of cholera in 1854 killed over 600 people. Cholera was believed to be carried in water. Dr. John Snow considered where people in the area were getting their water. They got their water from the same river—but in different places. Neither simple observations nor pure math and formal logic could lead the way past the impressionistic and speculative medicine of the time. But statistical reasoning could. Snow examined public pumps in the streets and *the rate of illness* in proximity to those pumps. It turned out that the water from only one pump was contaminated. People stopped drinking from that pump when Snow persuaded the local council to remove its handle, and the cholera epidemic came to an end.

A short time later, Florence Nightingale used statistical thinking to demonstrate that more soldiers were dying of infection during the Crimean War than from battle wounds (Cairo, 2019, pp. 175–81). Earlier, in 1847, Ignaz Semmelweis demonstrated that obstetricians washing their hands before delivering babies could save more infants' and mothers' lives.

No one more established the potency of these new statistical strategies than Sir Ronald Fisher (Matthews, 2018, pp. 53–55; Rubin, 1974). Fisher merged Galton's regression and Gauss's goodness of fit strategies (Fisher, 1922, pp. 597–612). He added numerous other tools considered foundational such as: p-values and significance tests, the power of a test (a measure of rejecting the null in favor of an alternative hypothesis given the alternative is true), and the power of an experiment (ability to detect a real effect as opposed to noise) (Spiegelhalter, 2020, p. 283). Finally, Fisher's textbook on research design is still in wide use (Fisher, 1971), and his work continues to affect the teaching of statistics (Silver, 2012, pp. 252–56).

Unlike theoretical justification in probability, which in the end is always proof-based, theoretical justification in statistics and research methodology is always an instance of ideas about what constitutes genuine knowledge and what is truly real (Wasserstein & Lazar, 2016, pp. 129–33). As statistician Nate Silver observed, "Information is no longer a scarce commodity; we have more of it than we know what to do with. . . . The [statistical] signal is the truth. The noise is what distracts us from the truth" (Silver, 2012, p. 17).

The real-world focus takes from calculus, probability, analytic geometry, and Boolean algebra only what is needed to accompany severe testing practices in the management of aggregated data. The master statistician's theories are at heart regulatory rules meant to preserve minimally biased representation of managed data by isolating informative signals from the noise omnipresent in data (Kahneman, Sibony, & Sunstein, 2021).

The Law of Figuring Things Out (LFTO) is a metaregulatory principle guiding regulatory principles that direct the use of mathematical tools for sorting and managing data. The LFTO is a component of rationality. It demands attention to the use of mathematical tools for constructing models that amplify human understanding and control over the world.

Epistemic champions of mathematics as described here are highly competent in mathematical application. They use this competency to improve inductive approaches to *reasoning about the world as it is*. A contemporary paradigm of this cadre of math champions is Judea Pearl. Pearl is no mere statistician. He is usually known as the father of computational Bayesianism. Certainly, this should suggest to the lay reader that he is both mathematically adept as a computer scientist and sensitive to the LFTO challenge of approximating ever better claims to know.

In a 2018 book, *The Book of Why: The New Science of Cause-and-Effect*, Pearl sets out to go beyond Bayesian approximations of truth to proposing mathematical formulas for discriminating among possible confounders and thereby identifying more of the causal paths of nature's arrangements. Pearl programs computers to identify and discard confounding factors and propose causal paths as a sort of "last man standing approach to induction." He uses massive amounts of algorithmic mathematics to get done what he intends computers to do for him.

So why is Pearl an epistemic champion of mathematics rather than an applied mathematician?

Pearl is not attempting to finalize the mathematical structure of reality. Instead, he wants to improve our best tools for approximating representation of reality. His work is hygiene for the human mind; it is not a matter of pulling back the curtain on nature's mathematical architecture. He exhibits endless zeal in his work; however, his adventures are not to seek beauty but to fashion an optimum model of investigatory thinking.

THE CROSSOVERS

Taxonomies are constructed by humans for human purposes. In any construction of taxonomies outside of pure mathematics there are nearly always candidates that do not seem to fit. So, we would like to suppose that our proposed taxonomy for illuminating personality traits reflects something of the collective personality of those who do mathematics. Hence, there is a need for a catch-all division. This grouping gathers those mathematicians who regularly seemed to cross over the above taxonomic divisions.

Already noted are people like the purist G. H. Hardy, who worked with the biologist Wilhelm Weinberg to create the Hardy-Weinberg law of genetic inheritance. But this was a rare foray for Hardy and one he seldom accepted praise for. Then there was the applied mathematician Blaise Pascal whose mathematics of wagering proved useful in making epistemic judgements, as he himself proposed in his famous theological wager. And finally, there was the epistemic mathematician, Judea Pearl, whose work in computer programming has been useful to applied mathematicians as much as it has been to epistemic sorts such as himself.

Setting aside those who only occasionally stepped into another area or found their work appropriated by others working with a different purpose in mind, there are still others whose careers seem always to keep them in more than one of the three areas of this taxonomy.

These include people such as the Santa Fe Institute's Stuart Kauffman, the great computer scientist Alan Turing, the mathematical game theorist John Nash, Gordon Moore of Moore's Law fame, and, perhaps most spectacularly, polymaths like Henri Poincaré and John von Neumann. In our treatment, we will discuss only one crossover exemplar: Benoit Mandelbrot.

Mandelbrot was born to two math teachers in Lithuania. He grew up a stone's throw from the then famed Warsaw University Mathematics center. In 1944 he took examinations to enter into doctoral programs in France's two premiere institutions in mathematics, the École Normale Supérieure and the École Polytechnique. He topped all candidates. He was a natural geometer and had formulaic intuitions similar to those the purist Ramanujan enjoyed (Mandelbrot, 2014).

For example, when considering a topic for his dissertation, he serendipitously came across linguist George Zipf's conjecture that there were statistical patterns one could detect in frequency of word usage. Mandelbrot's imagination was captured by the idea that there could be statistical patterns in such otherwise random data collections (Mandelbrot & Evertsz, 1990). This led him to focus on power-law relationships. Previous statistical practices paid little attention to data distributions not accounted for by standard Gaussian curves.

Mandelbrot was convinced that nature uses other distribution models than predecessors like Galton, Gauss, and Fisher could even imagine. Instead, nature sometimes uses power-law distributions of events. Mandelbrot showed that Zipf's conjecture applies not only to linguistic patterns but also to populations of cities, audiences for television shows, and annual incomes of people.

Eventually, Mandelbrot published articles on such pragmatic matters as the distribution of wealth, the stock market, thermodynamics, psycholinguistics, lengths of coastlines, fluid turbulence, population demographics, areas of islands, river networks, polymers, Brownian motion, random noise, and more. All this makes him sound like a candidate for a champion of applied mathematics! Not so fast.

Mandelbrot concluded that not only does nature abhor plane geometry's straight lines, but it disparages much of calculus's efforts at revelation as well. To accommodate nature, Mandelbrot conjured up the concept of a *fractal*. Fractals give a detailed structure on all scales of magnification. This all sounds very applied, but Mandelbrot was just as interested in journeying through novel territory in pure mathematics as he was showing novel ways of nature's layout of its furniture.

Mamdelbrot's creation of the Mandelbrot set in particular was sufficient to earn him the prize all purists seek, the Fields Medal—not just once but twice! He was also awarded the Wolf Prize (1993), the Légion d'Honneur, and the Japan Prize (2003).

Just as Mandelbrot was a champion in several areas representing mathematical champions consistently throughout his career, his appointment reflected similar multifaceted excellence. While he studied at places like California Institute of Technology and the École Polytechnique, he also served at the Institute for Advanced Study at Princeton and the Centre National de la Recherche Scientifique. All very purist. Yet he worked at IBM as a practical researcher for thirty-five years—very applied!

The psychological features of those who champion the mathematical quest should be apparent. Despite each mathematician having his or her own quirks and idiosyncrasies and interests, some personality traits seem to be definitive.

These champions are first and foremost *adventurers*. They each want to go where no one else ever had. They are not the sort of people who are likely to be manipulated to follow a crowd. They want understanding that is deep, personally secured, and properly owned within their own mind. Each champion has a zeal, a passion, embracing mathematics for its boundless gifts. Each exhibits both persistence and courage to continue their travelling through an intellectual wilderness despite the shadows and the lack of guideposts to follow.

Jacques Hadamard, E. T. Bell, and other earlier investigators into the personalities of mathematical accomplishment talk of beauty, harmony, and other features of math that stand outside the personality of math itself. Their focus is on characteristic of the discipline that may have attracted mathematical superstars. In contrast, our claim that the traits mathematicians bring with them before engaging in mathematical thinking are what help to make mathematics look so alluring when once it is truly encountered.

The personality complex of the champions taxonomized above shows, we believe, that understanding mathematical personality involves looking at both premathematical characteristics of those who thrive in its study as well as the problem fields of mathematics that marry so well with these human instincts for adventure and truth. With this in mind, we may discover many more students who can first love and then succeed in math than folk wisdom has previously allowed (Du Sautoy, 2003). The world needs math specialists, and not just specialists who utilize math in the service of other enterprises.

The ideal future would lead to more people who are very good in either applied math, pure math, epistemic math, or some combination thereof. Finally, there would be more champions of math in all three areas to serve as contemporary beacons of light illuminating ever widening and deeper paths in the great wildernesses of math.

KEY IDEAS OF CHAPTER 6

1. *Competency* catalogs many skills. In math it involves far more than mere talent for calculation. At the very least it involves *framing problems in productive ways* as much as, or more than, solving problems.
2. *The mathematical wilderness* can be entered from many directions and traversed in creative new ways every time. Proofs, formulas and theorems show explorers the way traversed.
3. The *collective personality* of mathematically minded people creates an instance of the Great Conversation of Humankind dedicated to exploring the mathematical wilderness.
4. *Beauty* can be found in a formula just as it is found in a piece of art. This beauty is in addition to its potency as a tool.
5. *The degree of understanding of the personality of math* by a student cannot be determined by analyzing a performance on a standardized multiple-choice test where the focus is simply on successful calculation.
6. *The Law of Figuring Things Out (LFTO) manifests human understanding.* Ideas, plans, and proofs cannot truly be understood in the absence of an architecture sufficient for an aptly framed problem. The LFTO is what explorers exploit to find their way into and about the mathematical wilderness.
7. *Exploring the mathematical wilderness is not magical.* It does not just happen to a person. All explorers, as is the case with all lovers, are in an important sense contributing to student-building (Wagner & Fair, 2020). With each new successful execution of the LFTO, the explorer learns more about how to navigate the contours and mysteries of the wilderness they love. Teachers who role- model commitment to the LFTO do more than any lecture or hands-on exercise to show what it means to seek and embrace a discipline such as math.
8. The Great Conversation of Humankind is the context within which student-building takes place in the lives of all who participate. The love for adventure, courage, and sustained commitment to pursue truth

animates the Great Conversation and disvalues settling for something merely good enough to get past the next math quiz.
9. One can become a *lover of math* without becoming an intellectual Olympian such as some of the men and women discussed throughout this book.
10. The *tyranny of multiple-choice tests,* beyond early warranted indoctrinative instruction, is an assault on student-building and hampers transit through thresholds requiring application of LFTO skills.

Chapter 7

Introducing Students to Mathematics

DON'T LEAVE OUT THE PERSONALITY!

Understanding the personality of mathematics involves understanding both the characteristic nature of math problems and understanding the personalities of math lovers. Math problems are provocative and alluring when well-framed. Math lovers stand in intimate juxtaposition with mathematics for their lifetime. The more these aspects of love for mathematics are understood, the more likely participation in mathematics opens for students at every level.

Greek antiquity produced math champions such as Zeno of Elea, Archimedes, Pythagoras, Plato, Thales of Meletus, Euclid, Eudoxus of Cnidus, Eratosthenes, Claudius Ptolemy, and Diophantus of Alexandria all between 546 BCE and 285 CE. And, significantly, around the world people with no knowledge of the Greeks or other's efforts, created mathematics *identical in structure* to that of the Greeks despite differences in culture and environments. Humans invent conventional symbols, but the structure of mathematics is unwavering.

Simone Weil and Lady Ada Lovelace were uncompromising in their love for math despite neither being able to accomplish what their mathematical heroes were able to do. In the case of Weil, it was her highly competent brother, André, and, in the case of Lady Ada, it was her mentor, Charles Babbage (Holt, 2018, pp. 169–70), who did what each could only hope to do. Still, each woman's love of math stayed with her until the end of her days.

The older students get, the more it seems they associate mathematical competency with a type of exotic nerdiness. That may be true of many of those most excellent in mathematics. Their zeal for exploring math may cause them to distance themselves from other, more worldly activities. But isn't this the case with lovers generally?

Infatuation leads folks to want to be alone with their beloved and away from distractions. Besides math zealots and lovers, the same could probably be said about the super high achievers in any discipline. Think of van Gogh's search for solitude to work. Think of the creator of analytic geometry, Descartes, locking himself away to think. Think of Wittgenstein, the wealthy aeronautical engineer and philosopher, hiding away in a cottage in Norway to write and think.

COMPETENCY FOR ALL

Competency is another matter. Competency encompasses a variety of skills distinguishing those who are able from those unable as well as those of extraordinary excellence.

Yet all from the competent and beyond can appreciate the allure of math once they identify more of its personality. For example, among the great mathematicians and the merely competent, both can appreciate awe in the presence of the mathematical wilderness.

As with any wilderness, the novice can enter from most anywhere. In the wilderness of math, one may enter intrigued by mysteries of the abstract such as imaginary numbers, infinities, geodesics outlining the "real" shape of worldly travel, tools that diminish noise from electronic gadgetry or diminish misleading inferences from "Big Data" that computers process.

The personality of math naturally invites investigation, but ineffective teaching and stifling cultural environments are liable to discourage the adventure. The champions of math share: a passion for adventure, a zeal for study, and courage to sustain study that brings to light vistas never before imagined.

A LAMENT FOR THOSE WHO MAY NEVER HAVE ENCOUNTERED THE PERSONALITY OF MATH

No one knows if she shares a propensity for pure math if she is never introduced to it. Mathematician Susan D'Agostino writes that she dropped out of math after failing a high school algebra exam. In college she went to an ashram in India to study yoga, and it brought her back to math. There is a beauty in mathematical contemplation she wanted to grasp (D'Agostino, 2020, p. 1). How one gets introduced to studies in math is incredibly relevant as to whether or not one will ever come to know math's personality (Su, 2020, pp. 79–83).

There are many creative programs that currently teach mathematical proficiency in the public schools, and some are quite good. The best of these programs should be expanded. These programs should be augmented by themes discussed in this book so that every student has a chance to experience math in a lively fashion. Initiating and preserving student interest in the subject may even reveal to some that there is a comfortable fit between their own personality and the personality of math (Wagner, 1982).

So, what is the collective personality of mathematically minded people? From the Renaissance on, Europe ascended to the pinnacle of mathematical activity. Of course, as the world advances further into what anthropologists are calling the Anthropocene Age, prominent mathematicians from Stanislav Smirnov to Maryam Mirzakhani and Elon Lindenstrauss, Fields and Abel Prize winners, come from the world at large and may live in places quite different from their ancestral home. For now, our attention will be on the champions of math in the Golden Age from the Renaissance to the twenty-first century.

Plato's allegory of the cave is meant to illustrate that the adventuresome mind can turn from what others settle for. The adventurer looks directly toward whatever may reveal truth. This is not a matter of free-thinking and creativity. It is an act of courage.

The unifying qualities of those excellent in mathematics are a sense of adventure and a capacity for awe and reverence in the presence of new discoveries. Euclid, Gauss, and Euler are often listed as the three greatest mathematicians. For many mathematicians, Euler's formula $e^{i p} + 1 = 0$ is the most beautiful of all formulas, at least on a par with Einstein's equation in physics: $e = mc^2$. Importantly, math educators today argue that "Euler's conceptual moves are more naturally aligned with students' natural intuitions, and thus easier to grasp than their standard contemporary counterparts" (Stipp, 2017, p. 167). In other words, some crowning achievements in mathematics may be at arm's reach and within the intuitive understanding of many high school students.

If math educators are right that Euler's derivation of the formula follows more naturally with student intuitions about such things as infinity, this highlights the idea that mathematical competency may, like linguistic expression, be far closer to capacities expressed in developing abilities of children. These natural intuitions are much in line with psychologist Howard Gardner's theory of Multiple Intelligences, especially as he explains it in his own life as well as his work through Harvard's Project Zero.

In the fashion of Jean Piaget, whose initial interest was in the logical and mathematical reasoning of his own children, so too Gardner began his investigation into intelligences by reflecting on his own encounters and in watching his children develop their own intelligences. Competency is far more accessible, it seems, than much standardized, rubric-driven research has found (Gardner, 2020). The main point of standardized tests may be simply to "crack the whip," to intimidate students to memorize text and listen in class. But cracking the whip is an indoctrinative strategy and must aim not at test results in the end but at the crossing of thresholds of understanding eventually.

THE ANSWER IS NOT IN TESTING AND EVEN LESS IN ALIGNING TEACHING TO TESTS

Focusing on relatively inexpensive standardized testing to measure what students have got in their heads tends to overlook what students have figured out or what they are not capable of figuring out. If they get the answer to a multiple-choice test question on the Pythagorean theorem when given, for example, that the sides of the right triangle are 3 and 4 respectively, by selecting multiple-choice item "C" that says 5 as the correct answer for the length of the hypotenuse, this may not indicate anything about their competency to apply the theorem to tile roofs, lay carpets, or do a host of other things the theorem is often used to accomplish.

Throughout this book and in previous work we tout what we call the Law of Figuring Things Out (LFTO). The Law of Figuring Things Out, we propose, is not about selecting answers on a multiple-choice test nor even about doing roofing, laying tile, or anything immediately solvable. Rather the LFTO is a metaregulatory tool. It reflects the idea that strategic rules of thinking can be acquired and then applied to lower-level rules applicable to specific problem-spaces at hand. This is why the LFTO finds such a natural home across the entire taxonomy of mathematical thinking.

The LFTO holds promise that rules for figuring things out can be conjured across math and other STEM studies and beyond. The LFTO must be supported by dispositions and attitudes, and it requires evolving intellectual skills and intelligences. For example, self-discipline and courage are needed to find regulatory protocols for figuring out a problem at hand. Certainly, perceptions of beauty and the excitement of inventing or discovering new insights are potent motivators, but they cannot be realized without bringing to bear the appropriate dispositional, attitudinal, and intellectual resources.

In much of education today, the flowering of the LFTO in students and the development of Gardner's intelligences may be affected by current social and professional attitudes toward the concept of work and fun. Consider first the attitudes so often swirling around the word "work." It is thought of as a burden. People go to work and then escape to enjoy life, often on the weekend, with a salary in hand. Students are often admonished to do their work before they can do something enjoyable later. In short, work is something that may all too often be felt as a burdensome necessity to be avoided when possible.

To put this social observation into more vivid context, ask yourself the question: what is the first job of every child? Answer: to become an adult. This is true not just of human children, but the young of all mammals. They role-model what they see again and again as they grow into adulthood. If the adults in their world rebel against things called "work," what would you expect observant children to conclude? If teachers do not like teaching math—as opposed to art or music or physical education—what attitude are their students likely to role-model?

In the case of nearly every math champion discussed, there was someone in their life who role-modeled joyful competency—it does not have to be excellence!—in regulating mathematical speculation. *Math work* was not despised. Instead, mathematical *challenges* were accepted as invitations to the thrill of adventure transiting one more threshold of understanding.

Look into a classroom where a teacher who does not like math talks to students about getting out their math homework to be corrected or getting out their math books to be instructed. The students are likely to mirror the teacher's attitude toward math and even more generally toward anything called work. Now imagine that same teacher beginning a class in art. She cheerily tells students to clear their desks as she hands out materials and tells them about the fun they are about to have. Many students smile with glee, free from work and with time for play. But does this contrast have to be? Is this contrast educationally productive in any way?

A PIAGETIAN-GARDNER MOMENT IN LOGICO-MATH INTELLIGENCE

One of the authors worried about such things when his oldest daughter was about to begin school. He set out on a Piagetian/Gardner program to see if he could make things different for her. To begin with, he tried always to speak about work he was doing around the house with a smile and an—at times feigned—eagerness to get to work on some project. When picking up his daughter from school each day from kindergarten on up through junior high, the conversation went as follows.

Dad: What did you do in school today?

Daughter: Nothing.

[Sound familiar?]

Dad: Did you have recess or get to play any new games in math?

[She was always told math is a game like Monopoly.]

Daughter: Yes, we did.

[And then she might elaborate on either something that happened at recess or something new in math.]

Dad: Did you do any art *work* today?

[Counting on the idea that teachers more often than not leap into an art lesson spiritedly, Dad could count on that being fun and so the word work need not acquire a demoralizing connotation.]

Did this strategy work?

In fourth grade, the elementary school had nothing more to teach her about math. So, the elementary school scheduled her for honors math on the other side of a large athletic field where there was an intermediate school. Not only did she excel in her math classes, but also, she was placed on the intermediate school's math team all three years to compete against other intermediate schools in the annual math contest between the district's intermediate schools. Was she a born genius? Not according to the standard IQ tests at the time. Rather she was simply free of adult role-modeling that disparaged work, math, and the combination of the two. Is this just one odd case?

A friend who had PhDs in both math and in English did the same with his son. By high school, his son was going to the University of Missouri-Kansas City for his math classes. Any runners reading this account may have heard of this young student. His name is Wesley Paul, and he held more than twenty long-distance running records on the international stage. What adults role-model to students does more than anything else to build zeal in students for an academic study, a hobby, or a sport.

THE LFTO REVISITED

The LFTO flowers in a community of inquiry where the conditions are established to enable what we have called the Great Conversation of Humankind. When students are *encouraged to search for problems,* instead of simply for answers, they are more likely to become reflective.

Extended reflection leads beyond mere answers to rules and protocols for arriving at well-framed challenges. Comprehending such rules and protocols leads to recognition that, while these may be problem-focused or discipline-focused, their existence depends upon an intuitive grasp that there are higher-level rules licensing, modifying, and restricting lower-level disciplinary rules. These higher-level rules comprise what we handily describe as the LFTO. The LFTO reigns over all disciplinary efforts to make sense of what exists. The LFTO reveals that intellectualizing is not a compartmentalized commodity—at least not initially.

Only when adventurers explore deep enough into the wilderness of a discipline does the need for regulatory rules become more apparent. Here is where novices first begin discovering the contours of the particular disciplinary wilderness. To explore this wilderness is to set out on an adventure of mastering previously unknown terrain. Understood in this fashion, math and other STEM studies can come to student minds as alluring as the social sciences or any of the arts.

In a previous work, we sketched the concept of *student-building* (Wagner & Fair, 2020). By student-building we mean preparing students for intellectual adventure. The intellectual adventure unfolds as students are welcomed into the Great Conversation of Humankind. This Great Conversation may take place in shared verbal give-and-take or through private reading of authors who have already made some headway into the wilderness of current student interest. Student-building is all about bringing students into the Great Conversation as active participants. It is a matter of moving away from indoctrination and transiting thresholds of understanding.

TRUTH IN THOUGHTS VS. TRUTH IN THINKING

America's oldest university, Harvard, has over its archways into the campus quad the university's motto "Veritas," Latin for truth. The university stands by its historic vision to welcome students into the serious pursuit of truth. Truths of any kind are answers. In contrast, entering into the "global university" we designate as the Great Conversation of Humankind has as its premise the LFTO. This is to say, participants are welcomed not on the premise of truth-finding, as the Harvard logo promises, but *on the premise of truth-seeking*. The LFTO is the foundation of the ultimate mission of thinking.

Thinking is an action. The purpose of the Great Conversation is not to lead novices through a museum of thoughts, but rather to employ thought as necessary to further figuring out how things stand in the world. The personality of mathematics is a vibrant center of this Great Conversation and is revealed in its tantalizing promise of adventure for each new entrant and potential zealot.

In the taxonomy of mathematical adventurers discussed previously we showed there was an allure in figuring out what was required to know a given sector of mathematics more intimately. Intimacy requires love and passion. So, it was unavoidable that the champions of the different taxonomic divisions fall in love with the adventure. Lovers are filled with zeal in their pursuit of the beloved. So it is with those most successful in pursuit of their beloved discipline. As historian Arturo Martinez explains in the case of the Pythagoreans, their love of the adventure became so encompassing, it led to a wholly cult-like collaboration and lifestyle (Martinez, 2012).

And just as one might idolize and love another from afar, so too many can become competent lovers and explorers of mathematics even if they never rise to the pinnacle of public excellence. Therefore, in addition to the inherent allure of mathematical ways of figuring things out, there is the additional allure of counting oneself among the lovers of math who exhibit the courage needed to take on the exciting adventure of blazing new trails into the inviting wilderness of mathematics.

Putting all this together, what does it all come to? When teachers understand that each discipline has a personality and that students are more likely to take to their studies as they become acquainted with the personality in friendly and comforting ways, then their success in learning is bound to increase. Thresholds are then sought by students themselves as measures of importance and achievement. When teachers know that, if they role-model a love for mathematics rather than disdain or, at best, mere tolerance for the work involved, then their students are more likely to warm to the adventure of mathematical investigation.

When teachers excitedly display the relevant personality traits of those who are champions of mathematics, when they exhibit traits of courage, self-discipline, and a passion for the adventure, this, together with the natural allure of mathematical challenges, can prompt some students to go farther. Such an approach can also inspire other students to step forward, however timidly, into the borders of the mathematical wilderness and, after they find nothing to fear, they may well find themselves moving toward a sustained mathematical competency.

Bringing students forward in the manner described above is how teachers can better build student competency in mathematics. Give students a chance to make friends with mathematics and her dearest enthusiasts. If teachers cannot find it in themselves to show such love and excitement for mathematics, then they should do everything possible to remove themselves from being charged with teaching the subject. Similarly, administrators must cooperate with teachers who cannot live up to the challenge by initiating protocols so those teachers can exit from the teaching of math.

Teachers who cannot warm to inviting students to learn not just facts but the personality of math and the dramatic accomplishments of its champions need to be removed from the math classroom for the good of the students. This may be a harsh saying, but teaching is about bringing students into the Great Conversation and not simply about providing jobs for adults who are ill-suited for the positions they occupy.

Finally, the tyranny of multiple-choice tests, which see the number of "correct" answers as the measure of all learning, must be dethroned, especially in mathematics. Mathematics, when properly understood, is perhaps more about thinking than any other discipline, save perhaps for philosophy. The LFTO should be the featured focus of attention in every math class at any age and not the anticipated score on some standardized test. The former invites shared adventure; the latter threatens the extinction of further investigation. Thresholds are achievements of relevance, not test performance which may be no more than artifacts testifying to exhaustive indoctrination.

And now, dear reader, the challenge is for us to decide what we can do to further, in ourselves and others, building a better, deeper acquaintance with the personality of math in those we are student-building. To the extent we educators succeed in doing this, our professional lives will be richer and our society better able to grasp important truths about the world. And, who knows how many new thresholds of math understanding we may transit during our student-building careers?

KEY IDEAS OF CHAPTER 7

1. *Traditional academic disciplines possess properties analogous to a human personality* such as allure, sociability, intensity, story-telling proclivities, demandingness, apt virtues of various kinds, and complexes of skills networked with problem-framing tendencies. Math is like this, but too often its personality is obscured from student sight except for those few who persevere into advanced specialist work.
2. *Math competency is available to nearly all*, but it is most likely to be acquired by those who have opportunities to study math in programs reflecting the spirit of the Great Conversation of Humankind.
3. *Ineffective teaching and stifling cultural environments* strip away all grounds for excitement when transiting thresholds leading to the wilderness of mathematics. The wilderness can be admired from afar by those merely or barely competent in math. But no one can understand anything about the wilderness when their vision has been blocked by *training programs* that do no more than force a handful of calculation practices on students.
4. You cannot like what you know nothing about. Taking students beyond necessary indoctrination to *threshold after threshold* is the path toward becoming at least very good at math or acquainted with aspects of its personality.
5. Schooling focused on training to pass standardized tests reinforces *a focus on shadows* people are trained to see.

6. *True math education brings out its disciplinary personality*, focusing on visions leading to transiting each new threshold. Thresholds open new insight and vistas of understanding, and utilizing the LFTO in the context of mathematical imagination leads to dreaming, not mere accounting.
7. *Doubt helps those engaged in student-building to escape complacency* and look forward to crossing a threshold into the light Plato described.
8. *You cannot teach students to love math by training them.* But you can model what love and understanding of math looks like if you genuinely love it yourself.
9. Computers can teach and learn, but *only qualified teachers can build students*.
10. *Veritas* is far more than a university slogan. It is the most important mission for any progressive society. Seeking and securing truth are vital to the core spirit, the personality of math.
11. *The Great Conversation of Humankind applies to math everywhere.* It crosses linguistic variants and number representation systems, and cultural, geographic, and historical borders are levelled in the Great Conversation of mathematics. From the Mayans to the Babylonians, from the Greeks to the people of China and India, from Euclid, Gauss, and von Neumann to Hypatia, Noether, and Mirzakhani, from astrophysicists like Hawking to gamblers and investors such as Ed Thorp, the Great Conversation welcomes all and embraces insights from every source that contributes to further understanding of the mathematical wilderness there for all to explore. Students have only to turn around and see the light.

Bibliography

Aczel, A. D. (2000). *The mystery of the aleph: Mathematics, the kabbalah, and the search for infinity.* New York, NY: Four Walls Eight Windows.
Aczel, A. D. (2011). *A strange wilderness: The lives of the great mathematicians.* New York, NY: Sterling Pub.
Aczel, A. D. (2015). *Finding zero: A mathematician's odyssey to uncover the origins of numbers.* New York, NY: St. Martin's Griffin.
Adkins, P. (2004). *Galileo's finger: The ten great ideas of science.* Oxford, UK: Oxford University Press.
Alexander, A. (2014). *Infinitesimals: How a dangerous mathematical theory shaped the modern world.* New York, NY: Scientific American/ FSG.
Al-Khalili, Jim. (2011). *The house of wisdom: How Arabic science saved ancient knowledge and gave us the Renaissance.* New York: Penguin Press.
Allman, G. (1976). *Greek geometry from Thales to Euclid.* New York, NY: Arno Press.
Alters, B. J. (1997). Whose nature of science? *Journal of Research in Science Teaching,* 34(1), 39–55.
Artstein, Z. (2014). *Mathematics and the real world: The remarkable role of evolution in the making of mathematics.* Amherst, NY: Prometheus Press.
Atteberry, A., & Mangan, D. (2020). The sensitivity of teacher value-added scores to the use of fall or spring test scores. *Educational Researcher,* 49(5), 335–49.
Baaz, M. et al., (eds.). (2011). *Kurt Gödel and the foundations of mathematics: Horizons of truth.* New York, NY: Cambridge University Press.
Bailey, R. (2010). Indoctrination. In R. Bailey, R. Barrow, & D. Carr, (eds.) *Sage handbook of philosophy of education.* London, UK: Sage Pub. Ltd.
Balter, M. (1998). Why settle down? The mystery of communities. *Science,* 282, 1442–46.
Bartha, P. (2010). *By parallel reasoning: The construction and evaluation of analogical arguments.* Oxford, UK: Oxford University Press.
Beckman, M. (2020). *Math without numbers.* New York, NY: Dutton.
Bell, E. T. (1957). *Men of mathematics.* New York, NY: Simon & Schuster.
Benbow, C., & Lubinski, D. (2007). Psychological profiles of the mathematically talented: Some sex difference and evidence supporting their biological bases. Chap.

4 In G. R. Block & K. Ackrill, (eds.) *The origins and development of high ability.* Ciba Foundation Symposium 178. https://doi.org/10.1002/9780470514498.

Berlinski, D. (1995). *A tour of the calculus.* New York, NY: Pantheon Books.

Berlinski, D. (2011). *One, two, three: Absolutely elementary mathematics.* New York, NY: Pantheon.

Bernoulli, J. (2006, original 1713). *Ars conjectandi.* Tr. E. D. Sylla as *The art of conjecturing, together with a letter to a friend on sets in court tennis.* Baltimore, MD: Johns Hopkins University Press.

Bhattacharya, A. (2022). *The man from the future: The visionary life of John von Neumann.* New York, NY: Norton.

Boesch, C., & Tomasello, M. (1998). Chimpanzee and human cultures. *Current Anthropology,* 39(5), 591–614.

Boyer, C. (1959). *The history of the calculus and its conceptual development.* New York, NY: Dover.

Boyer, C. (1968). *A history of mathematics.* New York, NY: Wiley.

Bradford, G. (2015). *Achievement.* New York, NY: Oxford University Press.

Bradley, J., & Howell, R. (2011). *Mathematics: Through the eyes of faith.* New York, NY: HarperOne.

Bressoud, D. M. (2019). *Calculus re-ordered: A history of the big ideas.* Princeton, NJ: Princeton University Press.

Brooks, M. (2021). *The art of more: How mathematics created civilization.* New York, NY: Pantheon.

Burge, T. (2010). *Origins of objectivity.* New York, NY: Oxford University Press.

Butterworth, B. (1999). *The mathematical brain.* London, UK: Macmillan.

Butterworth, B., & Kovas, Y. (2013). Understanding neurocognitive developmental disorders can improve education for all. *Science,* 340, 300–305.

Byers, W. (2007). *How mathematicians think: Using ambiguity, contradiction, and paradox to create mathematics.* Princeton, NJ: Princeton University Press.

Cairo, A. (2019). *How charts lie: Getting smarter about visual information.* New York, NY: Norton.

Callan, E., & Arena, D. (2009). Indoctrination. In H. Siegel (ed.), *The Oxford handbook of philosophy of education.* New York, NY: Oxford University Press.

Chinn, C.A., & Samarapungavan, A. (2011). Distinguishing between understanding and belief. *Theory into Practice,* 40(4), 235–41.

Chomsky N., & Robichaud, A. (2014). Standardized testing as an assault on humanism and critical thinking in education. *Radical Pedagogy,*11(1), 54–66.

Cobb, M. (2020). *The idea of the brain: The future of neuroscience.* New York, NY: Basic Books.

Coles, R. (1991). *The spiritual life of children.* San Francisco, CA: HarperOne.

Cook, M (2020). *Sleight of mind: 75 Ingenious paradoxes in mathematics, physics, and philosophy.* Cambridge, MA: MIT Press.

Courant, R. & Robbins, H. (1996). *What is mathematics? An elementary approach to ideas and methods.* New York, NY: Oxford University Press.

Crow, M. (1988). Ten misconceptions about mathematics and its history. In W. Aspray & P. Kitcher (eds.), *History and Philosophy of Modern Mathematics*. Minneapolis, MN: University of Minnesota Press.

Csibra, G., & Gergely, G. (2006). Social learning and cognition: the case for pedagogy. In Munkata, Y. & Johnson, M. (eds.), *Processes in Brain and Cognitive Development*. Oxford: Oxford University Press.

Csikszentmihalyi, M. (1988). The flow experience and its significance in human psychology. In Csikszentmihalyi, I. & Csikszentmihalyi, M. eds., *Optimal experience: Psychological processes of flow in consciousness* (pp. 15–35). New York, NY: Cambridge University Press.

Csikszentmihalyi, M. (1990). *Flow: The psychology of optimal experience*. New York, NY: Harper.

Curry, A. (2008). Seeking the roots of ritual. *Science*, 319, 278–80.

D'Agostino, S. (2020). *How to free your inner mathematician: Notes on mathematics and life*. New York, NY: Oxford University Press.

Darling-Hammond, L. (2007). Evaluating "No Child Left Behind." *The Nation*. Retrieved from http://www.thenation.com/article/evaluating-no-child-left-behind.

Dauben, J. W. (1990). *Georg Cantor: His mathematics and philosophy of the infinite* (2nd ed.). Princeton, NJ: Princeton University Press.

Davis, P. J., & Hersh, R. (1981). *The mathematical experience*. Boston, MA: Houghton-Mifflin.

Dedekind, R. (1888). *Was sind und was sollen die Zahlen*. Braunschweig, Deutschland: Friedr. Vieweg & Sohn. p. III.

DeFelipe, J. (2011). The evolution of the brain, the human nature of cortical circuits, and intellectual creativity. *Frontiers in Neuroanatomy*, 5 (May), Article 29.

Dehaene, S. (1997). *The number sense: How the mind creates mathematics*. New York, NY: Oxford.

Dehaene, S. (2009). Origins of mathematical intuitions: The case of arithmetic. *Annals of the New York Academy of Sciences*, 115, 232–59.

Dehaene, S. (2011). *The number sense: How the mind creates mathematics: Revised and updated edition*. New York: Oxford University Press.

Dehaene, S. (2020). *How we learn: Why brains are better than any machine . . . for now*. New York, NY: Viking.

Dehaene S., Dehaene-Lambertz, G., & Cohen, L. (1998). Abstract representations of numbers in the animal and human brain. *Trends in Neurosciences*, 21(8), 355–61.

Dehaene, S., Piazza, M., Pinel, P. & Cohen, L. (2003). Three parietal circuits for number processing. *Cognitive Neuropsychology*, 20(3), 487–506.

Derbyshire, J. (2004). *Prime obsession: Bernhard Riemann and the greatest unsolved problem in mathematics*. New York, NY: Plume Books.

Deutsch, D. (2009). A new way to explain explanation. TED Talk, minute 16:15, YouTube. https://www.youtube.com/watch?v=folTvNDL08A.

Deutsch, D. (2011). *The beginning of infinity*. New York, NY: Viking Press.

Devlin, K. (2000). *The math gene: How mathematical thinking evolved and why numbers are like gossip*. New York, NY: Basic Books.

Devlin, K. (2008). *The unfinished game: Pascal, Fermat and the seventeenth-century letter that made the world modern.* New York, NY: Basic Books.

Devlin, K. (2017). *Finding Fibonacci: The quest to rediscover the forgotten mathematical genius who changed the world.* Princeton, NJ: Princeton University Press.

Diaconis, P., & Skyrms, B. (2018). *Ten great ideas about chance.* Princeton, NJ: Princeton University Press.

Dreyfus, H., & Taylor, C. (2015). *Retrieving realism.* Cambridge, MA: Harvard University Press.

Du Sautoy, M. (2003). *The music of the primes.* New York, NY: Harper-Collins.

Du Sautoy, M. (2021). *Thinking better: The art of the shorcut in math and life.* New York: Basic Books.

Dzielska, M. (reprint, 1996). *Hypatia of Alexandria.* Cambridge, MA: Harvard University Press.

Elgin, C. Z. (2017). *True enough.* Cambridge, MA: MIT Press.

Ellenberg, J. (2014). *How not to be wrong: The power of mathematical thinking.* New York: Penguin Press.

Ellenberg, J. (2021). *Shape: The hidden geometry of information, biology, strategy, democracy, and everything else.* New York, NY: Penguin.

Ernest, P. (2006). A semiotic perspective of mathematical activity: The case of number. *Educational Studies in Mathematics,* 61(1–2), 67–101.

Erwig, M. (2017). *Once upon an algorithm.* Cambridge, MA: MIT Press.

Farmelo, G. (2019). *The universe speaks in numbers: How modern math reveals nature's secrets.* New York: NY: Basic Books.

Ferreiros, J. (2016). *Mathematical knowledge and the interplay of practices.* Princeton, NJ: Princeton University Press.

Feynman, R. (1985). *Surely you are joking, Mr. Feynman!* New York, NY: W. W. Norton.

Fisher, R. A. (1922). On the mathematical foundations of theoretical statistics. *Phil. Trans. R. Soc. Lond. A Containing Papers of a Mathematical or Physical Character* 222, 309–368.

Fisher, R. A. (1971). *The design of experiments* (9th ed.). New York, NY: Macmillan.

Fortnow, L. (2013). *The golden ticket: P, NP, and the search for the impossible.* Princeton, NJ: Princeton University Press.

Frenkel, E. (2013). *Love and math: The heart of hidden reality.* New York, NY: Basic Books.

Gallistel, C. R., Gelman, R., & Cordes, S. (2006). The cultural and evolutionary history of the real numbers. In S. Levinson & J. Pierre (eds.), *Evolution and culture,* pp. 247–74. Cambridge, MA: MIT Press.

Galton, F. (1887). Typical laws of heredity. *Nature* 15, 492–95, 512–514, 532–533.

Gardner, H. (2020). *A synthesizing mind: A memoir from the creator of multiple intelligences theory.* Cambridge, MA: MIT Press.

Gatchel, R. (1972). The evolution of a concept. In I. Snook (ed)., *Concepts of indoctrination,* pp. 2–22. New York, NY: Routledge.

Gigerenzer, G. (2002). *Calculated risk: How to know when numbers deceive you.* New York, NY: Simon and Schuster.

Gigerrenzer, G. (2015). *Risk savvy: How to make good decisions.* New York, NY: Penguin.

Glass, G. V. (2016). One hundred years of research: Prudent aspirations. *Educational Researcher*, 45(2), 69–72.

Glimcher, P. (2004, rev. ed.). *Decisions, uncertainty, and the brain.* Cambridge, MA: MIT Press.

Goldstein, R. (2005). *Incompleteness: The proof and paradox of Kurt Gödel.* New York, NY: Norton.

Gopnik, A., & Graf. P. (1988). Knowing how you know: Young children's ability to identify and remember the sources of their beliefs. *Child Development*, 59(5) (Oct.), 1366–1371.

Gopnik, A., Meltzkoff, M. A., & Kuhl, P. (1999). *The scientist in the crib: What early learning tells us about the mind.* New York: William Morrow Co.

Gordon P. (2004). Numerical cognition without words: evidence from Amazonia. *Science,* 306(5695), 496–99.

Gould, S. J. (1981). *The mismeasure of man.* New York, NY: Norton.

Graham, L., & Kantor, J-M. (2009). *Naming infinity: A true story of religious mysticism and mathematical creativity.* Cambridge, MA: Harvard University Press.

Gray, J. (2008). *Plato's ghost: The modernist transformation of mathematics.* Princeton, NJ: Princeton University Press.

Gray, J. (2012). *Henri Poincaré, a scientific biography.* Princeton, NJ: Princeton University Press.

Green, T. F. (1972). Indoctrination and beliefs. In I. A. Snook (ed.), *Concepts of indoctrination,* pp. 32–45. New York, NY: Routledge.

Hacker A. (2016). *The math myth: And other STEM delusions.* New York, NY: New Press.

Hacking, I. (1990). *The taming of chance.* New York, NY: Cambridge University Press.

Hacking, I. (2014). *Why is there philosophy of mathematics at all?* New York, NY: Cambridge University Press.

Hadamard, J. (1945). *The psychology of invention in the mathematical field.* Princeton, NJ: Princeton University Press.

Hales, T. (2008). Formal proof. *Notices of the American Mathematical Society*, 55(11),1370–81. Found at https://www.ams.org/notices/200811/200811–full-issue .pdf.

Halverson, H. (2020). *How logic works: A user's guide.* Princeton, NJ: Princeton University Press.

Hand, D. (2014). *The improbability principle.* New York, NY: Scientific American/Farrar, Straus & Giroux Press.

Hardy, G. H. (1967). *A mathematician's apology.* Cambridge, UK: Cambridge University Press.

Harris, M. (2015). *Mathematics without apologies.* Princeton, NJ: Princeton University Press.

Harvey, C. W. (2004). Liberal indoctrination and the problem of the community. *Synthese*, 111(1), 15–16.

Hauser, M. D., Chomsky, N., & Fitch, W. T. (2002). The faculty of language: What is it, who has it, and how did it evolve? *Science,* 298, 1569–1579.
Heard, J. (2019). *From servant to queen: A journey through Victorian mathematics.* New York, NY: Cambridge University Press.
Heaton, L. (2017). *A brief history of mathematical thought.* New York, NY: Oxford University Press.
Helms, S. J. (1980). *John von Neumann and Norbert Wiener: From mathematics to the technologies of death.* Cambridge, MA: MIT Press.
Hersh, R. (1997). *What is mathematics, really?* Oxford: UK: Oxford University Press.
Hersh, R. & John-Steiner, V. (2011). *Loving and hating mathematics: Challenging the myths of mathematical life.* Princeton, NJ: Princeton University Press.
Holt, J. (2018). *When Einstein walked with Gödel: Excursions to the edge of thought.* New York, NY: Farrar, Strauss & Giroux.
Hornstein, L. (2011). *The Tarskian turn: Deflationism and axiomatic truth.* Cambridge, MA: MIT Press.
Ifrah, G. (1985). *From one to zero: A universal history of numbers.* New York, NY: Viking.
Iliffe, R. (2017). *Priest of nature: The religious world of Isaac Newton.* New York, NY: Oxford.
Johnson, K., Hylick, J., & Moore, K. (2021). *Katherine Johnson: My remarkable journey.* New York, NY: Amistad.
Kahneman, D., Sibony, O., & Sunstein, C. (2021). *Noise: A flaw in human judgment.* New York, NY: Little, Brown Spark.
Kanigel, R. (1991). *The man who knew infinity.* New York, NY: Scribner.
Khaldun, I. (1989, original 14th century). *The Muqaddimah: An introduction to history.* Princeton, NJ: Princeton University Press.
Kjeldsen, T., et al. (2014). The role of history and philosophy in university mathematics education. In Matthews, M. (ed.), *International handbook of research in history, philosophy and science teaching,* pp. 837–871. Dordrecht, The Netherlands: Springer.
Kline, M. (1972). *Mathematical thought from ancient to modem times.* New York, NY: Oxford University Press.
Kneale, W., & Kneale, M. (1962, reprint 2008). *The development of logic.* New York, NY: Oxford University Press.
Kovalevskaya, S. (1978, original 1889). *A Russian childhood.* Translated, edited, and introduction by Beatrice Stillman. New York, NY: Springer.
Kovas, Y., Haworth, C. M., Petrill, S. A., & Plomin, R. (2007). Mathematical ability of 10-year old boys and girls. *Journal of Learning Disabilities,* 40, 554–67.
Koretz, D. (2008). *Measuring up: What educational testing really tells us.* Cambridge MA: Harvard University Press.
Koretz, D. (2017). *The testing charade: Pretending to make schools better.* Chicago, IL: University of Chicago Press.
Lakoff, G., & Nunez, R. (2000). *Where mathematics comes from.* New York, NY: Basic Books.

Landsman, J. & Gorski, P. (2007). Countering standardization. *Educational Leadership*, 64(8), 40–44.

Levitin, J. (2014). *The organized mind*. New York, NY: Dutton.

Lewis-Williams, D. & Pearce, D. (2005). *Inside the neolithic mind*. London, UK: Thames and Hudson.

Linden, D. J. (2020). *Unique: The new science of human individuality*. New York, NY: Basic Books.

Lockhart, P. (2017). *Arithmetic*. Cambridge, MA: Harvard University Press.

Lyons, I. M., & Beilock, S. L. (2011). Numerical ordering ability mediates the relation between number-sense and arithmetic competence. *Cognition*, 121(2), 256–261.

Mandelbrot, B. (2014). *The fractalist: Memoir of a scientific maverick*. New York, NY: Vintage.

Mandelbrot, B., & Evertsz, C. (1990). The potential distributions around growing fractal clusters. *Nature,* 348, 143–45.

Mankiewicz, R. (2000). *The story of mathematics*. Princeton, NJ: Princeton University Press.

Maor, E. (1991). *To infinity and beyond: A cultural history of the infinite*. Princeton, NJ: Princeton University Press.

Maor, E. (2019). *The Pythagorean theorem: A 4000–year history*. Princeton, NJ: Princeton University Press.

Marie-Pascale, N. (2005). Finger gnosia: A predictor of numerical abilities in children. *Child Neuropsychology,* 11, 413–30.

Martinez, A. (2011). Dividing by nothing. An entry from *Not Even Past, The Public Historian Blog* at the University of Texas. Retrieved from https://repositories.lib.utexas.edu/bitstream/handle/2152/81362/Dividing%20by%20Nothing%20–%20Not%20Even%20Past.pdf?sequence=2.

Martinez, A. (2012). *The cult of Pythagoras: Math and myths*. Pittsburgh, PA: University of Pittsburgh Press.

Massey, D. (2002). A brief history of human society: The origin and role of emotion in social life. *American Sociological Review,* 67, 1–29.

Mazur, B. (2008). Mathematical platonism and its opposites. *European Mathematical Society Newsletter*, 68, 19–21.

Mazur, J. (2016). *Fluke: The math and myth of chance and coincidence*. New York, NY: Basic Books.

Matthews, M., ed. (2018). *History, philosophy and science teaching*. Cham, Switzerland: Springer.

Mazur, J. (2005). *Euclid in the rainforest: Discovering universal truth in logic and math*. New York, NY: Pi Press.

Mazzotti, M. (2015). Maria Gaetana Agnesi, Mathematician of God. In S. Lawrence & M. McCartney (eds.), *Mathematicians and their gods*. New York, NY: Oxford University Press.

McKay, B., Bar-Natan, D., Bar-Hillel, M., & Kalai, G. (1999). Solving the bible code puzzle. *Statistical Science*, 14(2), 150–73.

Menninger, K. (1992). *Number words and number symbols: A cultural history of numbers*. Trans. P. Broneer. Mineola, NY: Dover Pub.

Mlodinow, L. (2015). *The upright thinkers: The human journey from living in trees to understanding the cosmos.* New York, NY: Pantheon Press.

Morris, I. (2015). *Foragers, farmers, and fossil fuels: How human values evolve.* Ed. Stephen Macedo. Princeton, NJ: Princeton University Press.

Morrison, K. (2022). Conceptual replications, research, and the "what works" agenda in education. *Educational Research and Evaluation,* 27(1–2), 35–60.

Nagel, E. & Newman, J. R. (2002). *Gödel's proof.* New York, NY: New York University Press.

Nahin, P. (2012). *The logician and the engineer: How George Boole and Claude Shannon created the information age.* Princeton, NJ: Princeton University Press.

Neale, V. (2017). *Closing the gap: The quest to understand prime numbers.* New York, NY: Oxford University Press.

Nehm, R., Kim, S., & Sheppard, K. (2009). Academic preparation in biology and advocacy for teaching evolution: biology versus non-biology teachers. *Science Education,* 93(6), 1122–46.

Neuenschwander, D. (2017, rev. ed.). *Emmy Noether's wonderful theorem.* Baltimore, MD: John Hopkins University Press.

Neyman, J. & Pearson, E. (1933). On the problem of the most efficient tests of statistical hypotheses. *Philosophical Transactions of the Royal Society of London. Series A, Containing Papers of a Mathematical or Physical Character,* 231, 289–337.

Nichols, S., Glass G., & Berliner, D. (2012). High-stakes testing and student achievement: Updated analyses with NAEP data. *Education Policy Analysis Archives,* 20(20), 1–30.

Nieder, A. (2019). *A brain for numbers: The biology of the number instinct.* Cambridge, MA: MIT.

Nieder, A., & Dehaene, S. (2009). Representation of number in the brain. *Annual Review of Neuroscience,* 32, 185–208.

Nirenberg, D., & Nirenberg, R. (2021). *Uncountable: A philosophical history of number and humanity from antiquity to the present.* Chicago, IL: University of Chicago Press.

Olsson, K. (2019). *The Weil conjectures: On math and the pursuit of the unknown.* New York, NY: Farrar, Strauss & Giroux.

Osterlind, S. (2019). *The error of truth: How history and mathematics came together to form our character and shape our worldview.* New York, NY: Oxford University Press.

Peano, G. (1889). *Arithmetices principia.* Turin, IT: Bocca.

Pearl, J. & Mackenzie, D. (2018). *The book of why: The new science of cause and effect.* New York, NY: Basic Books.

Pearl, J., Glymour, M., & Jewell, N. (2016). *Causal inference in statistics: A primer.* New York, NY: Wiley.

Pearson, K. (1900). X. On the criterion that a given system of deviations from the probable in the case of a correlated system of variables is such that it can be reasonably supposed to have arisen from random sampling. *The London, Edinburgh, and Dublin Philosophical Magazine and Journal of Science,* 50 (302), 157–175.

Perkins, D. N., Jay, E. & Tishman, S. (1993). New conception of thinking: From ontology to education. *Educational Psychologist*, 28, 67–85.

Peters, E. (2020). *Innumeracy in the wild: Misunderstanding and misusing numbers.* New York, NY: Oxford University Press.

Piazza, M., Pica, P., Izard, V., Spelke, E. S., & Dehaene, S. (2013). Education enhances the acuity of the nonverbal approximate number system. *Psychological Science*, 24, 1037–43.

Pica, P., Lemer, C., Izard, V., & Dehaene, S. (2004). Exact and approximate: arithmetic in an Amazonian indigene group. *Science*, 306(5695), 499–503.

Porter, T. M. (1986). *The rise of statistical thinking 1820–1900.* Princeton, NJ: Princeton University Press.

Posamentier, A. S. (2020). *The joy of geometry.* New York, NY: Prometheus Books.

Posamentier, A. & Spreitzer, C. (2020). *Math makers: The lives and works of 50 famous mathematicians.* Guilford, CT: Prometheus Books.

Poundstone, W. (1988). *Labyrinths of reason: Paradox, puzzles, and the frailty of knowledge.* New York, NY: Anchor Books.

Poundstone, W. (2019). *The doomsday calculation: How an equation that predicts the future is transforming everything we know about life and the universe.* New York, NY: Little, Brown Spark.

Putnam, H. (2015a). Naturalism, realism and normativity. *Journal of the American Philosophical Association*, 1(2), 312–28.

Putnam, H. (2015b). Intellectual autobiography of Hilary Putnam. In Auxier, R., Anderson, D., & Hahn, L. (eds.) *The philosophy of Hilary Putnam.* Library of Living Philosophers Volume XXXIV, pp. 3–110. Chicago, IL: Open Court.

Rashed, R. (2009). *Al-Khwarizmi: The beginnings of algebra.* London, UK: Saqi Books.

Ravitch, D. (2010). *The death and life of the great American school system: How testing and choice are undermining education.* New York, NY: Basic Books.

Richeson, D. (2019a). *Euler's gem: The polyhedron formula and the birth of topology.* Princeton, NJ: Princeton University Press.

Richeson, D. (2019b). *Tales of the impossible: The 2000-year quest to solve the mathematical problems of antiquity.* Princeton, NJ: Princeton University Press.

Ritchie, S. (2020). *Science fictions: How fraud, bias, negligence, and hype undermine the search for truth.* New York, NY: Metropolitan Books.

Rogers, B. (2003). Pascal's life and times. In N. Hammond (ed.), *The Cambridge companion to Pascal*, pp. 4–19. New York, NY: Cambridge University Press.

Rowlands, S. (2014). Philosophy and the secondary school mathematics classroom. In M. Matthews (ed.), *International handbook of research in history, philosophy, and science teaching*, pp. 705–730. Dordrecht, The Netherlands: Springer.

Rusconi, E., et al. (2005). Dexterity with numbers: rTMS over left angular gyrus disrupts finger gnosis and number processing. *Neuropsychologia* 43, 1609–24.

Sandifer, E. (2007). *How Euler did it.* Washington, DC: Mathematical Association of America.

Schwarzlose, R. (2021). *Brainscapes: The warped, wondrous maps written in your brain—and how they guide you.* New York, NY: Houghton-Mifflin.

Secolsky, C., Judd, T., Magaram, E., Levy, S., Kossar, B., & Reese, G. (2016). Using think-aloud protocols to uncover misconceptions and improve developmental math instruction: An exploratory study. *Numeracy*, 9(1), Article 6.

Segerstrale, U. (2013). *Nature's oracle: The life and work of W. D. Hamilton.* New York, NY: Oxford University Press.

Seife, C. (2000). *Zero: Biography of a dangerous idea.* New York, NY: Viking Penguin.

Shannon, C., & Weaver, W. (1949). *The mathematical theory of communication.* Urbana, IL: The University of Illinois Press.

Siegel, H. (1988). *Educating reason: Rationality, critical thinking, and education.* New York: Routledge.

Siegel, H. (1989). Relativism refuted: A critique of contemporary epistemological relativism. *British Journal of Philosophy of Science*, 40(3), 419–27.

Siegel, H., & Smith, M. U. (2019). Must evolutionary education that aims at belief be indoctrinating? *Science and Education*, 28(9–10), 1235–47.

Sigman, M. (2017). *The secret life of the mind.* New York, NY: Little, Brown & Co.

Silver, N. (2012). *The signal and the noise: Why so many predictions fail—but some don't.* New York, NY: Penguin.

Singh, S. (1997). *Fermat's enigma: The epic quest to solve the world's greatest mathematical problem.* New York, NY: Walker and Company.

Skyrms, B. (2014). *Social dynamics.* New York, NY: Oxford University Press.

Smith, G. (2014). *Standard deviations: Flawed assumptions, tortured data, and other ways to lie with statistics.* London, UK: Overlook Duckworth, Peter Mayer Publications, Inc.

Snook, I. A. (1970). The concept of indoctrination. *Studies in Philosophy of Education* 7(2), 65–108.

Snook, I. A. (ed.) (1972). *Concepts of indoctrination.* London, UK: Routledge & Kegan Paul.

Sober, E. (2015). *Ockham's razors: A user's manual.* Cambridge, UK: Cambridge University Press.

Sokal, A. (2009). *Beyond the hoax: science, philosophy and culture.* Oxford, UK: Oxford University Press.

Soni, J., & Goodman, R. (2017). *A mind at play: How Claude Shannon invented the information age.* New York, NY: Simon & Schuster.

Sosa, E. (2011). *Reflective knowledge: Apt belief and rational knowledge.* Oxford, UK: Oxford University Press.

Spelke, E., Breinlinger, B., Macomber, J., & Jacobson, K. (1992). Origins of knowledge. *Psychological Review*, 99(4), 605–32.

Spiegelhalter, D. (2020). *The art of statistics: How to learn from data.* New York, NY: Basic Books.

Stewart, I. (2013). *Visions of infinity.* New York, NY: Basic Books.

Stewart, I. (2017). *Significant figures: The lives of great mathematicians.* New York, NY: Basic Books.

Stewart, I. (2021). *What's the use: How mathematics shapes everyday life.* New York, NY: Basic Books.

Stigler, S. (1989). Francis Galton's account of the invention of correlation. *Statistical Science*, 4(2), 73–86.
Stillwell, J. (2019). *Reverse mathematics: Proofs from the inside out.* Princeton NJ: Princeton University Press.
Stipp, D. (2017). *A most elegant equation: Euler's formula and the beauty of mathematics.* New York, NY: Basic Books.
Strogatz, S. (2019). *Infinite powers: The calculus reveals the secrets of the universe.* New York, NY: Houghton Mifflin.
Su, F. (2020). *Mathematics for human flourishing.* New Haven, CT: Yale University Press.
Suppes, P. (1962). *Towards a behavioral foundation of mathematical proofs.* Technical Report No. 44, Psychology series, Institute for Mathematical Studies in the Social Sciences, Stanford University.
Suppes, P. (1965). On the behavioral foundations of mathematical concepts. *Child Development Monograph Serial* 99, 30(1), 60–96.
Suppes P. (1970). *A Probabilistic Theory of Causality.* Amsterdam, The Netherlands: North-Holland Publishing Co.
Suppes, P. (1984). *Probabilistic metaphysics.* London, UK: Blackwell.
Taleb, N. (2007). *The black swan: The impact of the highly improbable.* New York. NY: Random House.
Taleb, N. (2020). *Statistical consequences of fat tails: Real world preasymptotics, epistemology, and applications.* New York, NY: STEM Academic Publishers.
Tammet, D. (2012). *Thinking in numbers: How maths illuminates our lives.* London, UK: Hodder & Stoughton.
Tent, M. (2008). *Emmy Noether: The mother of modern algebra.* Wellesley, MA: A. K. Peters / CRC Press.
Thackray, A., Brock, D., & Jones, R. (2015). *Moore's law: The life of Gordon Moore, Silicon Valley's quiet revolutionary.* New York, NY: Basic Books.
Thorp, E. O. (2017). *A man for all markets.: From Las Vegas to Wall Street, How I beat the dealer and the market.* New York, NY: Random House.
Tomasello, M. (2001). *The cultural origins of human cognition.* Cambridge, MA: Harvard University Press.
Tomasello, M. (2014). *A natural history of human thinking.* Cambridge, MA: Harvard University Press.
Treffers, A. (1991). Meeting innumeracy at primary school. *Educational Studies in Mathematics,* 22(4), 333–52.
Tversky, B. (2019). *Mind in motion: How action shapes thought.* New York, NY: Basic Books.
Wagner, P. A. (1980a). A philosophical approach to mathematics education. *Proceedings of the Thirty-sixth Annual Meeting of the Philosophy of Education Society,* (36), 376–83.
Wagner, P. A. (1980b). Metamathematical aspects of science and science education of the future. In Rudd, K. & Harkins, A. (eds.), *Educational Decisions: Studies for the Future Sourcebook II,* pp. 240–47. Minneapolis, MN: World Future Society.

Wagner, P. A. (1981). Conceptual change, rationality and philosophy of education. *Scientia* 116, Annus LXXXV, 669–80.

Wagner, P. A. (1982). The philosopher as teacher: Philosophy in mathematics education. *Metaphilosophy*, 13(1), 79–90.

Wagner, P. A. (1986). Philosophical praxis. *Teaching Philosophy*, 9(4), 291–99.

Wagner, P. A. (2006). Probability, decision theory, and a curriculum for better thinking. *Journal of Thought*, 41(2), 23–38.

Wagner, P. A. (2011). Isolationism and the assault on the possibility of shared truths. *Interchange,* 42(4), 389–408.

Wagner, P. A. (2018). Warranted indoctrination in science education. In Matthews, M. (ed.), *Handbook in history and philosophy of science education.* Dordrecht, The Netherlands: Springer.

Wagner, P. A. (2021). The methods, benefits and limitations of indoctrination in mathematics education. *Interchange: A Quarterly Review of Education*, 52(1), 41–56.

Wagner, P. A., & Dede, C. (1983). Disciplinary paradigm shifts: A new frontier for future researchers. *World Future Society Bulletin*, XVII (2), 25–29.

Wagner, P. A., & Fair, F. (2020). *Education for knowing: Theories of knowledge for effective student building.* Lanham, MD: Rowman & Littlefield.

Wagner, P. A., & Freedman, G. (1985). Legitimate classes of evidence for identifying effective teaching, *Journal of Thought*, 20(2), 35–49.

Wagner, P. A., Johnson, D., Fair, F., & Fasko, D. (2017). *Focus on thinking.* Lanham, MD: Rowman & Littlefield.

Wagner, P. A., Johnson, D., Fair, F., & Fasko, D. (2018). *Thinking ahead.* Lanham, MD: Rowman & Littlefield.

Wagner, R. (2012). Infinity metaphors, idealism, and the applicability of mathematics. *Iyyun: The Jerusalem Philosophical Quarterly*, 61(2), 129–48.

Wagner, R. (2017). *Making and breaking mathematical sense: Histories and philosophies of mathematical practice.* Princeton, NJ: Princeton University Press.

Wang, H. (1987). *Reflections on Kurt Gödel.* Cambridge, MA: MIT.

Wang, H. (1996). *A logical journey.* Cambridge, MA: MIT Press.

Wasserstein R. L., & Lazar, N. A. (2016). The ASA's statement on p-values: context, process, and purpose. *The American Statistician,* 70, 129–33.

Watts, E. (2017). *Hypatia: The life and legend of an ancient philosopher.* New York, NY: Oxford University Press.

Weinstein, M. (2013). *Logic, truth and inquiry.* London, UK: College Publications.

Wheeler M., & Feghali, I. (1983). Much ado about nothing: Preservice elementary school teachers' concept of zero. *Journal of Research in Math Education*, 14, 147–55.

Wiley, R. (2015). *Noise matters: The evolution of communication.* Cambridge, MA: Harvard University Press.

Wittgenstein, L. (1975). In C. Diamond (ed.), *Lectures on the foundations of mathematics.* Ithaca, NY: Cornell University Press.

Wright, S. (1921). Correlation and causation. *Journal of Agricultural Research*, 20, 557–585.

Wynne, J. (2021). *Do Not Erase: Mathematicians and Their Chalkboards.* Princeton, NJ: Princeton University Press.

Yau, Shing-Tung & Nadis, S. (2019). *The shape of a life: One mathematician's search for the universe's hidden geometry.* New Haven, CT: Yale University Press.

Zellini, P. (2020). *The mathematics of the gods and the algorithms of men: A cultural history* (trans. S. Carnell & E. Segre). New York, NY: Pegasus.

Zermelo, E. (1904). Proof that every set can be well-ordered. English translation, pp. 139–141 in J. van Heijenoort (ed.), 1967, *From Frege to Gödel: A source book in mathematical logic 1879–1931.* Cambridge, MA: Harvard University Press.

Index

abstraction, 7–8, 16
Acta Mathematica, 59
Agnesi, Maria Gaetana, xvi, 48, 55–56, 85
Alexandria, xvi, 41–44, 43–44
algebra, 72, 87–88, 94
algorithms, 53, 87–88
Anthropocene Age, 103
Apollo 13 (film), 13
applied math, xvi–xvii, 49, 51–54, 87–91, 95–98
apt teaching, 19–20, 30
archaeology, 69
Archimedes, 71
arguments, 82–83
Aristotle, xiv, 19, 28, 42
arithmetic, 11
art, xiii, 22, 78
artificial intelligence, 68–69
astronomy, 45
Atomic Energy Commission, 33
Axiom of Choice, 73
axioms, 67, 73, 92

Babbage, Charles, 56–57, 60
Babylon, 7, 42, 56
Bayes, Thomas, 8, 47–48
beauty, 30, 98
beliefs, 3–4

Bell, E. T., 41, 84, 97
Benbow, Camelia, 54–55
benchmarks, 4–5, 14–16
Benedict XIV (pope), 48, 55
Bernoulli family, 89
Bhattathiri, Melpathur Narayana, 88
Big Data, 102
biographies, 63
biology, 69
The Book of Why (Mackenzie and Pearl), 95
Boole, George, 38
Boolean algebra, 94
botany, 57
Bourbaki Group, 73
Brahe, Tycho, 45
Brahmagupta, 66–67
brains, 6, 37–38, 70
Brazil, 65–66
Bryn Mawr College, 62
Byron (Lord), 56–57, 60
Byron, Ada, 56–57, 60, 62, 101

calculations: with computers, 50; efficiency of, 37; for Humankind, 33; with infinity, 26–27; learning, 8–9; by students, 31; with triangles, 71; understanding for, 16
calculus, 27–28, 72, 89

Cambridge University, 34–35
Cantor, Georg, 72–73, 81
Carroll, Lewis, 63
challenge, 64, 105
champions, 80–84, 92–95, 97, 101. *See also* heroes
cherry-picking strategies, 40–41
children: communication with, 19; culture of, 3–4; intelligence of, 31; Judaism for, xiii; learning by, 103–4; reading for, 50; teaching, 48, 105–6
China, 42, 88
cholera, 94
Christianity, 41–42
Chung, Catherine, 57–58
Cobb, Matthew, 13
Coles, Robert, xiv
collective personality, 98
communication, 15–16, 19
community, 22
competency, 98, 101–4, 102, 109
computers, 32, 50, 52–54
concepts: awareness of, 102–4; of Euler, 103; in geometry, 70–71; of heroes, 33–34; misconceptions, 3; provocative, 74–75; regression to the mean, 93; student-building, 107; in theology, 70; threshold, 9–11, 14–16; with zero, 49–50
Confucius, xiii
context-driven fundamentals, 7–8, 14
continuums, 72–73
Copernicus, 45, 84
correlation coefficient r, 93
counting, 65–66, 81–82
Csikszentmihalyi, Mihaly, 39
cubic equations, 74–75
culture: Agnesi in, 55–56; of Alexandria, xvi, 41–44, 43–44; of children, 3–4; engagement with, 65–66; in Europe, 59; history of, xiii–xiv; Humankind and, 60–61; in Middle East, 45; physics and, 20–21; of Pythagoreans, xiii, 7, 21, 42, 108;

Pythagorean Theorem in, 66; race in, 53–54; women in, 62–64
Curie, Marie, 62
curiosity, 39
curriculum, 2

D'Agostino, Susan, 102
Darwin, Charles, 58
da Vinci, Leonardo, xiii
Dedekind, 67
Dehaene, Stanislas, 37–38, 77
De Morgan, Augustus, 62–63
Descartes, René, 75, 102
Deutsch, David, 46, 90
Devlin, Keith, 33–34, 53
diagonals, 71
Diophantus, 66–67
division, 82–83
Dodgson, Charles, 63
Do Not Erase (Wynne), 52
Dostoevsky, Fyodor, 58
doubt, 14–17, 67, 110
Du Sautoy, Marcus, 36, 39–41
École Normale Supérieure, 96
École Polytechnique, 96–97

education: challenge in, 105; gender in, 54–63; higher, 32, 34–35, 37, 58–60; honesty in, 49; from indoctrination, 4–5; in Islam, xiii; learning and, 14–16; math, xv–xvii, 11–13; personalities in, 75–76; philosophy in, xiv–xv; psychology of, 78; in school, 49, 104–5; of students, 1–3; theory and, 79–80; traditional, 109
Egorov, Dmitri, 85
Egypt, 7, 41–42
Einstein, Albert, 34–35, 40, 60, 90
Elements (Euclid), 23
Elgin, Catherine, 7
engagement, xvii, 13, 28, 65–66, 101–2
engineering, 9, 13, 38
Enlightenment, 66, 75
epidemiology, 93–94
epistemology, 49, 92–96

Erdös, Paul, 34, 36
Euclid, 21, 28; axioms of, 92; Fifth Postulate of, 36, 43, 66–67, 73; for geometry, 42–43; geometry to, 85; to mathematicians, xvi–xvii, 23–24, 36; reputation of, 57, 60–61
Euler, Leonhard, 36, 57, 59–61, 82–84, 103
Europe, 44–45, 56, 59, 88
evolution, 56, 78–79
experiential feelings, 30
exploration, 36–37

Faraday, Michael, 63
Fermat, Pierre de, 46–47, 58, 89, 92
Feynman, Richard, xiv–xv, 37
Fibonacci numbers, 45, 78
Fifth Postulate, 36, 43, 66–67, 73
finger notation, 65–66
Fisher, Ronald, 94
Florensky, Pavel, 85
fractals, 96–97
France, 73
Freedom 7 mission, 54–55
Frenkel, Edward, xiii
fundamentals, of math, 7–8, 14, 22–23

Galileo Galilei, 28, 45–46, 89, 92
Galton, Francis, 62–63, 93
Gardner, Howard, 103–4
Gauss, Carl, 8, 34–36, 38–39, 57–58, 60–61, 84, 92
gender, 54–63
genetics, 56–57
geniuses, 31, 33–34
geometry, 23–24, 36, 42–43, 85; concepts in, 70–71; in Greece, 56, 71; hypotheses in, 73; knowledge of, 75
Germain, Sophie, 58, 64
Germany, 61–62
Gigerenzer, Gerc, xiv
Glimcher, Paul, 77–78
God, 46–48
Gödel, Kurt, 48, 70, 81, 85–86

Gould, Stephen J., 2
Graduate Record Exam, 40
gravity, 28
Great Conversation: of Humankind, xiv–xv, 11, 15–16, 64, 98, 106–7, 110; learning from, xvii; students in, 109; thinking with, 9
Greece, 7, 23, 42; champions from, 101; China and, 88; geometry in, 56, 71; LFTO in, 83–84; proofs in, 66

Hacking, Ian, 5–6, 79
Hadamard, Jacques, 97
Halverson, Hans, 90
Hamilton, Richard, 22
Hardy, G. H., xvi, 34, 53–54, 87, 95
Hawking, Stephen, 39
heroes, 33–34, 35–38, 41–49, 55, 76
higher education, 32, 34–35, 37, 48, 58–60
Hilbert, David, xvi, 8, 25–26, 61, 73, 86–87
Hilbertian Hotels, xvi, 8, 25–26, 27
history: of abstraction, 7; of computers, 53–54; of counting, 65–66; cultural, xiii–xiv; of evolution, 78–79; heroes in, 41–49; of indoctrination, 3–4; of math, 77–79; of mathematical schooling, 5–9; mathematicians in, xvi–xvii, 19–23, 35–38, 57
History of Mathematics (Bell), 41
honesty, 41–43, 49
Howard, Ron, 13
Humankind: Aristotle for, 19; brain development for, 6; calculations for, 33; culture and, 60–61; Great Conversation of, xiv–xv, 11, 15–16, 64, 98, 106–7, 110; human number processing, 49; learning about, 35; personalities and, 52–53; physics for, 54; psychology of, 73; taxonomies of, 81; thinking and, 5–6; understanding and, 48–49
Hume, David, 92
Huxley, Thomas, 58

Huygens, Christian, 46
Hypatia, xvi, 41–42, 55, 63
hypotheses, 73

imaginary numbers, 48, 66–67, 71–72, 74–75
imagination, 5, 9, 24–25
Incompleteness Theorems (Gödel), 70
India, 43–44, 88
indoctrination, xv–xvi, 3–5, 14–16, 19–20
inductive inferences, 92
ineffective teaching, 109
infinitesimals, 82–83
infinity, 24, 26–27, 29–30, 70–74
intelligence: geniuses, 31, 33–34; intellectual freedom, xiv–xv, 14–17; of mathematicians, 38–39; of Perelman, 86–87; personalities and, 59–60; testing, 106; Theory of Multiple Intelligences, 103–4; understanding and, 49
intentionality, 78
International Congress of Mathematics, 72–73
investigation, 30
Ioannidis, John, 2
Islam, xiii, 66–67
Italy, 56, 67, 75

Jaleel, Aliya, 63
Johnson, Katherine, 54–55
Judaism, xiii

Kauffman, Stuart, 96
Kepler, Johannes, 45, 84
Keynes, John Maynard, 92
Khayyam, Omar, 44
al-Khwarzimi, Muhammed ibn Musa, 44, 66–67, 87–88
"Kiatab al jabr w'al-muqabala" (al-Khwarzimi), 44
knowledge, 5, 40–41, 49, 57, 75, 92
Komolgorov, Andrey, 92
König, Julius, 72–73

Kovalevskaya, Sofia, xvi, 58–60, 64, 86

Lagrange, Joseph-Louis, 59
language, 6, 22, 32–33, 46, 75
Lao Tzu, xiii
Laplace, Pierre-Simon, 89
Law of Figuring Things Out (LFTO), 83–84, 94–95, 98, 104–7, 110
Law of Large Numbers, 74
learning: arithmetic, 11; calculations, 8–9; with cherry-picking strategies, 40–41; by children, 103–4; from curiosity, 39; education and, 14–16; from Great Conversation, xvii; with honesty, 41; about Humankind, 35; with imagination, 24–25; with indoctrination, 19–20; language, 6; with LFTO, 104–7; with love, 23, 30; math, 16; with passion, 2; in religion, 85; in school, xv, 3–4; with symbols, 6–7; thinking and, 31; threshold concepts, 9–11, 14–16; with transparency, xvi
Legendre, Adrien-Marie, 92
Leibniz, Gottfried, 8, 27, 45–46, 88–89
Leonardo of Pisa, 44–45
LFTO. *See* Law of Figuring Things Out
Lindenstrauss, Elon, 103
Liu Hui, 88
logic, 44–45
love, 23, 25–26, 30, 99, 107–8, 110
Love and Math (Frenkel), xiii
Lovell, Jim, 13
Luzin, Nicolai, 85

machine thinking, 52
Mackenzie, D., 95
Mallory, George, 64
Malthus, Thomas, 51
Mandelbrot, Benoit, 36, 96–97
Marr, David, 13
Martinez, Arturo, 108
Maryam's Magic (Reid and Jaleel), 63
math. *See specific topics*

mathematicians: abstraction by, 8; applied math to, 87–91; diversity of, xvii; Euclid as, xvi–xvii, 23–24, 36; in history, xvi–xvii, 19–23, 35–38, 57; infinity for, 29–30; intelligence of, 38–39; knowledge to, 40–41; LFTO to, 83; Newton to, 8, 27–28; personalities of, 41–49; philosophy of, 95–98; proofs to, 73; psychology of, 32–35; pure math to, 84–87; scientists and, 2–3, 51–52; thinking by, 53–54; women as, 57–62; Zeno to, xvi, 26–27
Max Planck Institute for Human Development, xiv
McClintock, Barbara, 57
Mersenne, Marin, 68–69
Mesopotamia, 6–7
metaphysics, xiv
Middle East, 45, 88
Mill, John Stuart, 92
Mirzakhani, Maryam, 34, 63–64, 103
misconceptions, 3
Moore, Gordon, 96
Morgenstern, Oscar, 33, 88
multiplication, 82

Nambudiri, Parameshvara, 88
NASA, 13, 54–55
Nash, John, 2, 39, 96
nature, 88–89
Neale, Vicky, 68
negative numbers, 75
Nekrasov, Nikolay, 74
neuroeconomics, 77–78
neuroscientists, 5–6, 13, 34–35, 37–38
Newton, Isaac, 8, 27–28, 45–46, 84, 88–89, 91
Nieder, Andreas, 78
Nightingale, Florence, 94
No Child Left Behind Act, 5
Noether, Emmy, 60–63, 60–64, 86
numbers: beauty in, 30; counting, 6, 65–66, 81–82; Fibonacci, 45, 78; human number processing, 49; imaginary, 48, 66–67, 71–72, 74–75; imagination of, 24–25; infinity, 24, 26–27, 29–30, 70–74; Law of Large Numbers, 74; negative, 75; number sense, 16; number theory, 49, 61, 76; pi, 79, 85, 88; prime, xvi–xvii, 67–68; problems with, 65–66; to Ramanujan, 36; zero, 49–50, 82–83
numerals, 45
numerical representation, 16

On Calculations (al-Khwarzimi), 44, 87–88

Parallel Postulate, 67
Pascal, Blaise, 8, 46–47, 89, 91–92, 95–96
Paul, Wesley, 106
Peano, Giuseppe, 63, 67, 70
Pearl, J., 95
Pearl, Judea, 95, 96
Pearson, Karl, 62–63, 93
pedagogy, 2
Perelman, Grigori, 2, 22, 34, 43, 85–87
personalities: in education, 75–76; to Gauss, 38–39; Humankind and, 52–53; intelligence and, 59–60; of mathematicians, 41–49; psychology of, 29–30; teaching, 101–2
personality, of math. *See specific topics*
philosophy, xiv–xv, 32–33, 45–48, 95–98
physics, 20–21, 38, 45–46, 54, 69
pi, 79, 85, 88
Picard, Charles-Emile, 73
Picasso, Pablo, xiii
Pirahã tribe, 65–66
Plato, 7–8, 21–23, 28, 81; to Dehaene, 37–38; geometry to, 43; pure math to, 84–85; reality to, 67; truth to, 103
Poincaré, Henri, 22, 96
politics, 5, 57–64, 61–62
prejudice, 54–55
prime numbers, xvi–xvii, 67–68
Prix Bordin, 59

probability, 80, 90–91
problems, 65–75, 86–87
problem spaces, 13, 25–26
proofs, 12; fundamentals from, 22–23; in geometry, 42; in Greece, 66; knowledge from, 49; to mathematicians, 73; for problems, 66–67; by women, 58
provocative concepts, 74–75
psychology: of champions, 97; of education, 78; in higher education, 37; of Humankind, 73; of intelligence, 39; of love, 107–8; of mathematicians, 32–35; math in, 5–6; to neuroscientists, 34; of personalities, 29–30; in school, 38; of standardized testing, 1–2, 16; of students, 8–9; of threshold concepts, 15
pure math, xvi–xvii, 49, 51–54, 84–87, 95–98
pyramids, 78
Pythagoreans, xiii, 7, 21, 42, 79, 108
Pythagorean Theorem, xv, 12, 23, 66, 88, 104

race, 53–54
Ramanujan, Srinivasa, xvi, 33–35, 33–36, 86
Ramsey, Frank, 92
reading, 50
refugees, 61–62
regression to the mean, 93–94
regulatory principles, 94–95
Reid, Megan, 63
religion, 46–48, 55–56, 85
Renaissance, 56
Republic (Plato), 21
research, 11, 34–35, 103–4
Riemann, Bernhard, 90
rules, 21–22
Russia, 73–74

SATs, 1

school: art in, xiii; education in, 49, 104–5; indoctrination in, xv–xvi; learning in, xv, 3–4; logic in, 44–45; math in, 5–9, 53; in Mesopotamia, 6–7; psychology in, 38; STEM subjects in, 1–2, 20; students in, 104–5; testing in, 109
science, 55–57, 69, 88–89, 92. *See also specific sciences*
scientists, 2–3, 5–6, 14, 19–21, 34–35, 51–52
Semmelweis, Ignaz, 94
Sen, Amartya, xiii
Seurat, Georges, 92
Shannon, Claude, xvi, 2, 32–33, 40, 84, 90–91
Shephard, Alan, 54–55
Shing-Tung Yau, 2
Silver, Nate, 94
Smirnov, Stanislav, 103
Snow, John, 94
Socrates, xiii, 21
solutions, 68–70, 74–75, 104
Somayaji, Nilakantha, 88
Spiegelhalter, David, 92
sports, 72
square roots, 12–13, 66–67, 75
standardized testing, xv–xvi, 1–2, 5, 16
statistics, 2–3, 90–91, 94
STEM subjects, 1–2, 20, 60, 63–64, 104, 107
students: calculations by, 31; champions to, 80–84; competency of, 101–2, 109; education of, 1–3; engagement with, xvii, 28, 101–2; exploration by, 36–37; in Great Conversation, 109; indoctrination of, 3–4; infinity to, 24; psychology of, 8–9; Pythagorean Theorem to, 12; in school, 104–5; student-building, 107; teaching, 9–11, 14–16, 77; testing of, xiv–xv; truth to, 110
Su, Francis, 78
subtraction, 82
Summers, Larry, 54–55

Suppes, Patrick, xvi, 32–33
symbols, 6–7, 66

Tarski, Alfred, 61–62
taxonomies, 81, 95–96
teaching: apt, 19–20, 30; to benchmarks, 4–5; children, 48, 105–6; Computer-Assisted Instruction, 32; efficacy in, 37; ineffective, 109; love, 110; personalities, 101–2; procedures for, 11–12; students, 9–11, 14–16, 77; teachable moments, xvii; testing and, 104–5; thinking, 8–9
technology, 35, 68–69
The Tenth Muse (Chung), 57–58
testing: Graduate Record Exam, 40; intelligence, 106; in school, 109; standardized, xv–xvi, 1–2, 5, 16; of students, xiv–xv; teaching and, 104–5; tyranny of, 99, 109
theology, 46, 70
theory: Axiom of Choice, 73; education and, 79–80; evolution, 56; Fermat's last theorem, 58; of gravity, 28; Incompleteness Theorems, 70; number, 49, 61, 76; Pythagorean Theorem, xv, 12, 23; rules and, 21–22; theoretical justification, 94; Theory of Multiple Intelligences, 103–4
thinking: by brains, 70; after communication, 15–16; with epistemology, 49; with Great Conversation, 9; Humankind and, 5–6; learning and, 31; machine, 52; math, 78; mathematical, 43; by mathematicians, 53–54; statistical, 94; teaching, 8–9; tools for, 9–10; truth in, 107–9; about zero, 44
Thorp, Edward, 90–91
threshold concepts, 9–11, 14–16

transparency, xvi, 20
triangles, 71, 104
truth, 42–43, 47–48, 103, 107–10
Tsu Ch'ung Chih, 88
Turing, Alan, 39, 53, 96
Tversky, Amos, 2
Tversky, Barbara, 78

understanding, 11, 13, 16, 30, 48–49, 98
University of Bologna, 48
University of Göttingen, 59

van Gogh, Vincent, 102
Venkatesh, Akshay, 34
von Neumann, John, xvi, 2, 33, 36, 62, 88, 96

Wagner, Paul, 32
Wainer, Howard, 2–3
Weiertrauss, Karl, 59
Weil, Simone, 101
Weinberg, Wilhelm, 95
Wiener, Norbert, xvi, 53–54, 87
Wiles, Andrew, 58
women: in culture, 62–64; in higher education, 48, 58–60; Hypatia, 41–42; in math, xvi, 48, 54–57; as mathematicians, 57–62; proofs by, 58; in STEM subjects, 60, 63–64
World War II, 61–62
Wright, Sewall, 62–63
Wynne, Jessica, 52

Young Sheldon (TV show), 39

Zeno, xvi, 26–27, 28
Zermelo, Ernst, 73
zero, 44, 49–50, 82–83
Zipf, George, 96
zygotes, 19, 21

About the Authors

Paul A. Wagner is the senior ranking faculty member at the University of Houston—Clear Lake. He is chair of the Department of Leadership and Policy Analysis, which includes all research methodologies, statisticians, and educational administrative faculty. He also holds a joint appointment in the College of Human Sciences and Humanities. He has also taught management theory and organizational behavior for University of Houston–Victoria School of Business and consulted in strategic planning in several major corporations and universities. He is a member of the American Philosophical Association, the American Psychological Association, and the American Educational Research Association. He has formerly served as executive secretary of the Philosophy of Education Society, and vice president of the Association of Philosophers in Education (a division of the American Philosophical Association). He has authored more than one hundred publications, including this one, his tenth book.

Frank Fair is a Distinguished Emeritus Professor in the Department of Psychology and Philosophy at Sam Houston State University. He served for a number of years as the coordinator of the Philosophy Program in the department, and he was managing editor of the journal *INQUIRY: Critical Thinking Across the Disciplines* from 2010 until his retirement from full-time teaching in 2017. His presentations and publications span a wide range of topics from issues in logic and philosophy of science to survey research on the impact of post-tenure review policies in Texas, and from affirmative action to Buddhism and Christianity in relation to modern science. With a coauthor, he has written an article about listening to Plato for a quality management journal, and with the same coauthor he wrote a business fable that is a response to Spencer Johnson's classic "cheese book." He coauthored with Paul Wagner and two other colleagues three books on employing Philosophy for Children (P4C) in the classroom, and again with Paul the book *Education for Knowing*. But what he most values is a collaboration with colleagues to replicate in an American school district a Scottish study of the positive impact of one-hour-per-week P4C discussion sessions on several classes of seventh graders' cognitive abilities. And the students' cognitive gains were still visible in the data three years later when they were high school sophomores!

www.ingramcontent.com/pod-product-compliance
Lightning Source LLC
Chambersburg PA
CBHW021759230426
43669CB00006B/132